Brian Halloran
Boston June 1992

別冊商店建築58

ニューヨーク
ホテル&レストラン

NEW YORK hotels & restaurants

斎　藤　武

別冊商店建築58

ニューヨーク ホテル&レストラン

目次

●レストラン&ホテル名の後の番号はマップのものと同じです。

●名データ・レストラン&ホテル名・所在地・電話番号・料金等は本書取材時のものです。変更されている場合もありますので、ご了承ください。　1991年10月 商店建築社

NEW YORK hotels & restaurants

Contents

●No.after each restaurant & hotel name is same as that on the map.

●Data, such name, telephone No. and price described on the book, denote those as of the time when they were collected. They may have changed thereafter. Kindly understand such change.

October 1991 Shotenkenchiku-sha

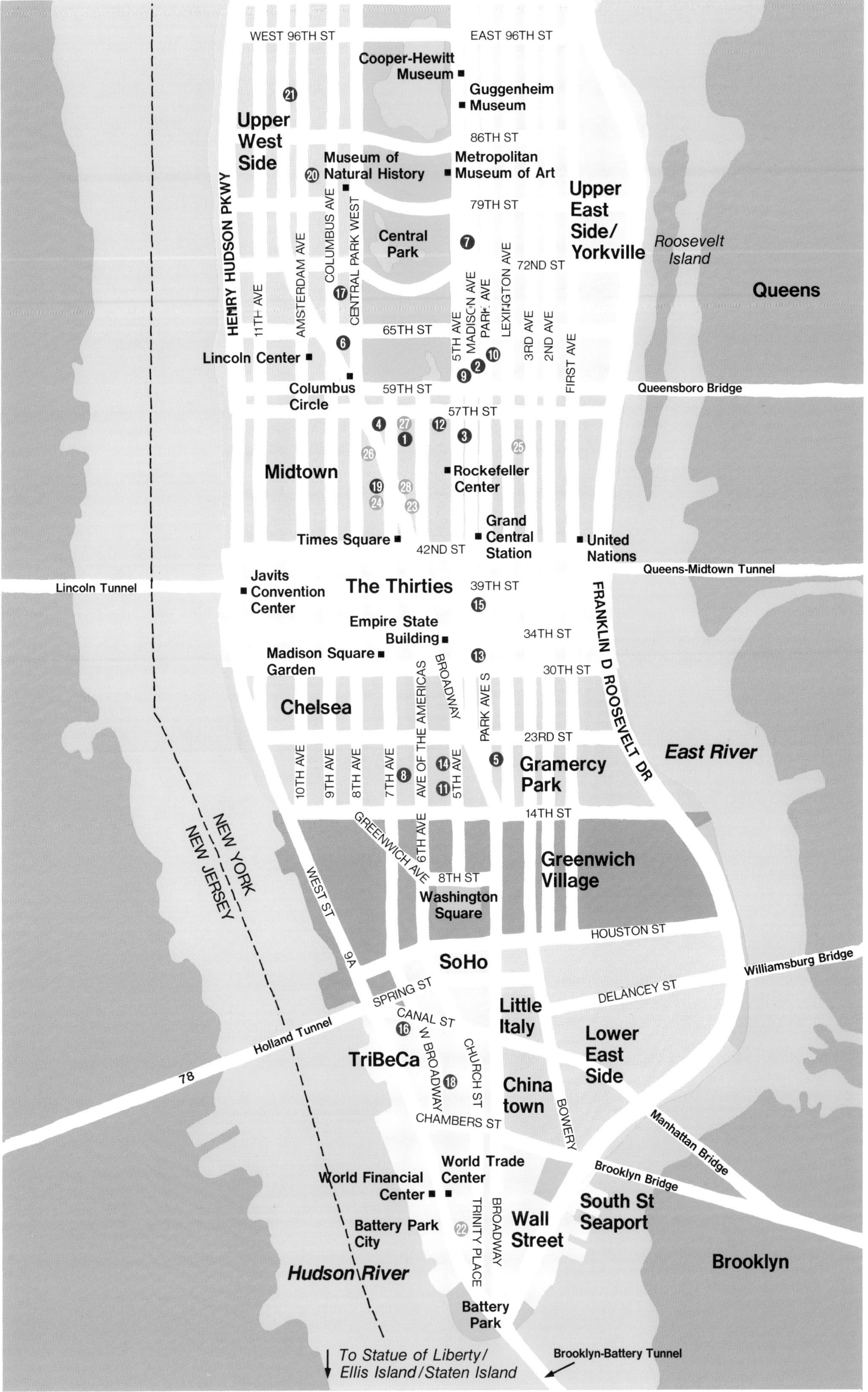

WEST 96TH ST
EAST 96TH ST
Cooper-Hewitt Museum
Guggenheim Museum
Upper West Side
86TH ST
Museum of Natural History
Metropolitan Museum of Art
Upper East Side/ Yorkville
79TH ST
HENRY HUDSON PKWY
Central Park
Roosevelt Island
72ND ST
Queens
11TH AVE
AMSTERDAM AVE
COLUMBUS AVE
CENTRAL PARK WEST
MADISON AVE
PARK AVE
LEXINGTON AVE
65TH ST
5TH AVE
3RD AVE
2ND AVE
FIRST AVE
Lincoln Center
Columbus Circle
59TH ST
Queensboro Bridge
57TH ST
Midtown
Rockefeller Center
Grand Central Station
Times Square
42ND ST
United Nations
Queens-Midtown Tunnel
Lincoln Tunnel
Javits Convention Center
The Thirties
39TH ST
FRANKLIN D ROOSEVELT DR
Empire State Building
34TH ST
Madison Square Garden
BROADWAY
30TH ST
AVE OF THE AMERICAS
Chelsea
PARK AVE S
23RD ST
East River
10TH AVE
9TH AVE
8TH AVE
7TH AVE
Gramercy Park
14TH ST
NEW YORK
NEW JERSEY
GREENWICH AVE
6TH AVE
Greenwich Village
WEST ST
8TH ST
Washington Square
HOUSTON ST
9A
SoHo
Williamsburg Bridge
SPRING ST
DELANCEY ST
Little Italy
CANAL ST
Holland Tunnel
Lower East Side
W BROADWAY
CHURCH ST
TriBeCa
78
China town
BOWERY
CHAMBERS ST
Manhattan Bridge
World Trade Center
Brooklyn Bridge
World Financial Center
South St Seaport
TRINITY PLACE
Battery Park City
Wall Street
Brooklyn
Hudson River
Battery Park
To Statue of Liberty/ Ellis Island/Staten Island
Brooklyn-Battery Tunnel

はじめに

世界で最もエキサイティングな都市の一つがニューヨークである。人類のるつぼと云われ、様々な文化が交差し新しいものが続々と創りだされている。今回はこのニューヨークにフォーカスをしぼり、注目され、話題となっているレストランとホテルを取材した。いずれも1990年前後にオープンした新しいものが中心である。しかしながら、この両業界にとっては非常に厳しい時期となり、リセッションやバブルの崩壊といった背景の中で今まで以上に苦戦を強いられている。特にこの一年間はその影響が顕著で、取材して半年もたたないうちに閉店の憂目に追い込まれたレストランも何軒かあった。いずれもすばらしいデコアやシェフの作る料理であったが、敢えてここでの収録を見合わせた。ここに収録されたレストランやホテルは幸いにも、この最終原稿を入稿する段階のチェックでは健在であり、末永く健闘されるよう願っている。

特筆すべきは、アメリカ生まれのシェフたちの活躍が大変目立ち始めてきたこと。これまでは多くの調理人をヨーロッパから迎えてきたが、ここにきてその世代交代の動きが見えてきた。アメリカの地方料理に関心が持たれるようになったのもその現れの一つだし、ニューイングランドやサウスウエスタン料理の人気がたかまり、調理法としては、グリルが盛んになってきた。

店舗デザインにかけるコストや面積はややスローダウンの傾向がうかがえ、大きな投資を避けた小規模のレストランが見立つ。有名な高級レストランは相変わらず繁盛しているが、一般的にはビストロやカフェ・パブといったカジュアルなレストランで、ライトでヘルシィな食事をとり、外食費をおさえる傾向といった業界の見方もあるようだ。

ホテルに関しては、ビジネス トラベラーを第一のターゲットとし、他には観光客やウィークエンドの利用客のためのパッケージプランなどにも力を入れている。最先端のビジネス機器の客室への導入も一般化し会議室の空気を一時間に5回も入れ替える設備を持つホテルも現れた。スイート型ホテルが増えてきたのもホテルライフの大きな革命といえる。より機能的でゆったりと過ごせる空間が求められている今、アメニティ性を付加することで売上の安定と増加をめざしているといえよう。

最後に本書をまとめるにあたり、取材に応じていただいた各ホテル・レストラン・そして、アメリカの代表的な設計家Adam D. Tihany氏、レストランのセレクト及び取材のために情報を提供していただいたニューヨーク在住のレストランコンサルタント、Leslie Holland氏、月刊「飲食店経営」編集部ほか、関係各位の協力に対し感謝いたします。

1991年10月

フォトジャーナリスト 斎藤 武

FOREWORD

One of the most exciting cities in the world is New York. Called a melting pot of races, New York features various types of culture intermingling with each other, and creates one novel thing after another. Focusing on New York, I have collected data on restaurants and hotels which are drawing attention and frequently talked about. All of them have opened recently – primarily in 1990 and 1991. However, both types of businesses encountered a very hard time, and are experiencing more hardships than ever, reflecting the recession and the collapse of the "bubble" economy. These influences have been exerted noticeably during the past year, and there were a number of restaurants which had unfortunately to go out of business within less than half a year from the time when I collected the respective data. Although these restaurants featured wonderful decor and dishes cooked by the chef, I eschewed from introducing them in the book. Fortunately, when the final manuscript was delivered, the restaurants and hotels covered by the book remain in normal operation according to my check, and I hope that they continue to prosper for as long a time as possible.

It deserves special mention that the activities of chefs born in America are beginning to become conspicuous. So far, many cooks have been invited from Europe. At present, however, a change of generation is taking place. One such sign is an increasing interest in American local foods, and New England and Southwestern foods are gaining in popularity. As a cooking method, using a grill is becoming popular.

The cost and areas secured for shop designs are showing a small downturn, and small-sized restaurants opening without much investment are noticeable. Although well-known high class restaurants remain prosperous, in the eyes of trade people, there seems to be a customer tendency towards having a light and healthy meal at casual restaurants such as bistros, cafes and pubs, in order to cut down on dining out expenses.

Now, a look at hotels shows that they are endeavoring to capture business travellers as the primary target, and provide package plans for tourists and weekenders. It has also become a common practice to install state-of-the-art business equipment in guest rooms, and even a hotel which replaces conference room air 5 times an hour. Increases in suite type hotels may be said to be a major revolution in hotel life. Now that a more functional and comfortable space is demanded, hotels are pursuing more stable and increased sales by equipping themselves with amenities.

In closing, let me say my heart-felt thanks to the hotels and restaurants which kindly responded to my request for data, Mr. Adam D. Tihany, a representative restaurant designer in the USA, and Miss Leslie Holland, a restaurant consultant living in New York, for her assistance and insight in selecting the restaurants I photographed. My thanks also go to the editorial department of the monthly "Inshokuten Keiei" and all those concerned for their cooperation.

October 1991

Gen Takeshi Saito
Photo Journalist

Published by **Shotenkenchiku-sha Co., Ltd.**
7-22-36-2, Nishi-shinjuku, Shinjuku-ku, Tokyo
160 Japan

Printed in Japan

別冊商店建築58 **ニューヨーク** ホテル&レストラン 1991年11月15日発行

著者 斎藤 武　編集●辻田 博　協力スタッフ　本文レイアウト●ぱとおく社　印刷●小堀グラフィックス　製本●坂田製本
編集発行人 村上末吉　制作●菅谷良夫　表紙デザイン●ウィークエンド　英文●海広社　写植●福島写植　山田製本

発行所 株式会社商店建築社©
本社 東京都新宿区西新宿7-22-36-2 〒160 TEL 03(3363)5770代 支社 大阪市中央区西心斎橋1-9-28 第3大京ビル 〒542 TEL 06(251)6523代
ISBN4-7858-0019-4

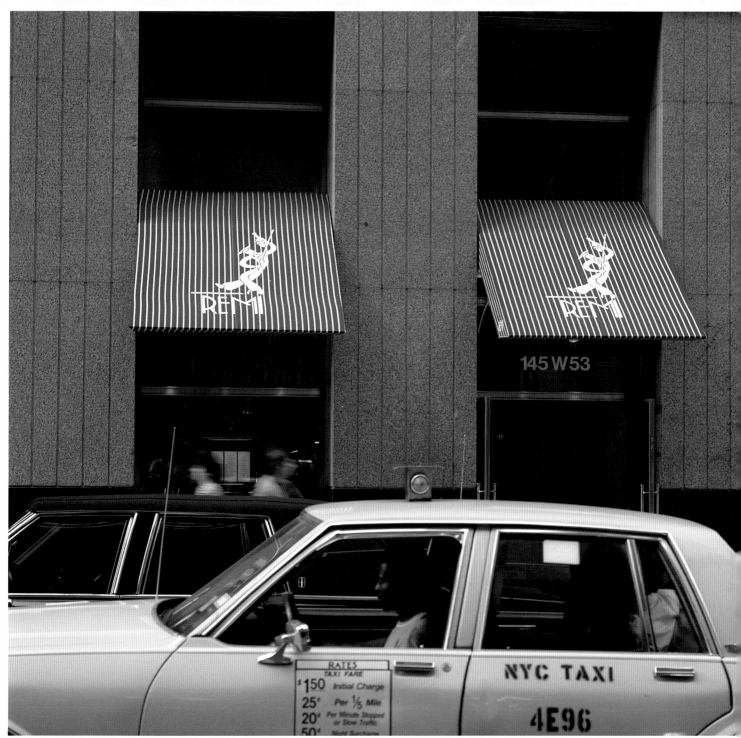

53rdストリートのウエストサイドに位置するファサード　ゴンドラのオールを漕ぐ人をロゴにしている

The facade which moved to the West Side of the 53rd Street; featuring a logo of a gondola oarsman.

145 West 53rd Street New York, N.Y. 10019
Phone/212-581-4242

右/広い空間をもったレセプション廻り

Right / The spacious reception area.

ベニスのシーンを演出した店内　幅約36m　120度に展開する壁画が店内いっぱいに描かれ　レストランの新しい空間デザインの表現として話題となっている

The interior presenting a Venice scene; the fresco, painted for about 36 m long and in 120 degrees, is drawing attention as a new-type design using the restaurant space.

レミ

アメリカを代表する空間デザイナー　アダム　ティハニー(Adam D.Tihany)自らが設計プロデュースし　経営するイタリアンレストラン。店名の「レミ」とは　水の都ヴェニスに浮かぶゴンドラのオールのことで　天井のデザインに生かされている。高い天井空間の店内には120フィートの大きな壁画をとり入れて　ニューヨーカーたちをアッと言わせた。パリ生まれのアーティスト　ポウリン　パリ(Paulin Paris)のヴェニスのイメージ風景画で　客席にすわると　まるでヴェニスの運河に浮かぶゴンドラから見る風景を想わせるというねらいだ。

料理は　アップスケールのイタリア料理で　アンティパスト　魚　パスタ　肉料理などで構成されるメニューは　37種類(ディナーメニュー)に限定し　客単価をグラスワインを含めてランチ約20ドル　ディナー40ドルに設定している。

開店　：1990年6月11日
営業時間：正午～午後2時30分(ランチ)
　午後5時30分～11時30分(ディナー)
客席数　：160席　テラス70席　バー10席
従業員　：80名
客単価　：ランチ/20ドル　ディナー/40ドル(グラスワイン含む)

REMI

This Italian restaurant was designed, constructed and managed by Adam D. Tihany, a leading American space designer in his own right. The shop name "Remi" means an oar of a gondola floating on the water in Venice, the city of water, and an image of an oar is used in the ceiling design. The interior which has a high ceiling, startled New Yorkers when a huge 120 feet fresco was installed. It is a landscape of Venice painted by Paulin Paris, an artist born in Paris. When seated inside, one can enjoy a scene as if viewed from a gondola floating on a canal in Venice.

The dinner menu is composed of only 37 types of upscale Italian food, such as antipasto, fish, pasta and meat dishes. The average price per customer is set at about $20 for lunch and $40 for dinner, including a glass of wine.

Opened : June 11, 1990
Hours : noon to 2:30 p.m. (lunch)
5:30 p.m. to 11:30 p.m. (dinner)
Capacity : 160 seats, terrace 70 seats, bar 10 seats
Number of employees: 80
Price per customer : lunch/$20, dinner/$40 (including a glass of wine)

共同経営者のデザイナー・Adam D. Tihany氏とシェフ・Francesco Antonucci氏

Adam D. Tihany, designer and joint manager, and Francesco Antonucci, chef.

34才のアーティスト・Paulin Paris氏による壁画はベニスのファンタジーをテーマに描き　その下には幾何学形の燭台をイメージしたライトが連なってテーブル席にやわらかい光を放っている

The fresco painted by Paulin Paris, 34-year-old artist, took up a fantasy of Venice as a theme, and lights imaging geometrical candles are arranged in a row beneath the fresco, casting a soft light over the table seating area.

店内のテーブル席が小さく見えるほど迫力を感じさす壁面空間の演出

The wall space presentation; so impressive that the inside table seating area looks small.

テーブル席はちょうどゴンドラに乗っている位置で　その上方に運河の橋脚とベニスの風景が見えるといった見事な演出だ
The table seating is placed just at a level onboard the gondola so that, as if sitting on the gondola, guests can enjoy viewing the piers of a bridge across a canal and a scene of Venice – a wonderful presentation.

イタリア産のブランデー・Grappaのコレクションを飾った柱を利用したサービス ステーション
The service station utilizing pillars on which a collection of Italian brandy "Grappa" is displayed.

店内中央部に設けられたサービス ステーション
The service station provided in the center of the interior.

ベネチアン シャンデリアや18世紀のムラノ グラス(Murano glassware)を配したバーエリア
The bar area accented with Venetian chandeliers and Murano glassware in the 18th century.

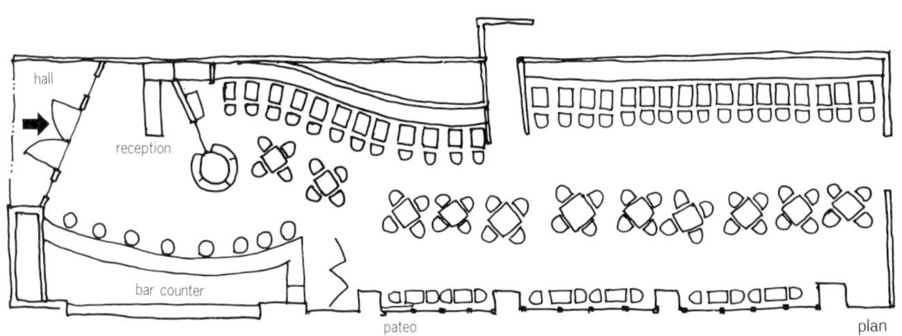

右/入口近くに曲線カウンターを設けたマホガニーのバー

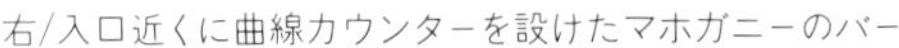

Right / The mahogany bar equipped with a curved bar near the entrance.

シェフ・F.Antonucciを中心に オードブルからデザートまで全てが地下のキッチンで作られる
All items from hors d'œuvre to dessert are cooked at an underground kitchen mainly by the chef F. Antonucci.

①

②

③

④

1/ ANITRA ALL'AGRODOLCE
Breast of Duck with Sweet and Sour Balsamic Vinegar Sauce and Carrot Mustard

2/ GOLOSEZI ALLA VENEZIANA
Assortment of Homemade Cookies and Sweets

3/ INVOLTINO DI POLLO CON SCAMORZA E ZUCCHINI
Rolled Chicken Breast Filled with Smoked Mozzarella and Zucchini, Served with a Leaf Salad

4/ TONNO AI SAPORI DEL MEDITERRNEO
Sauteed Rare Tuna with Garlic, Rosemary and Tomatoes

地中海の夜 光 波などを表現する店内の演出 バーカウンターの上方20フィートの高さの天井空間にティハニー氏がデザインした鉄と銅製のシャンデリアがある

The interior presentation expressing the nocturnal light, waves, etc. on the Mediterranean Sea; on the ceiling space 20 feet high above the bar counter one finds iron & copper chandeliers designed by Tihany.

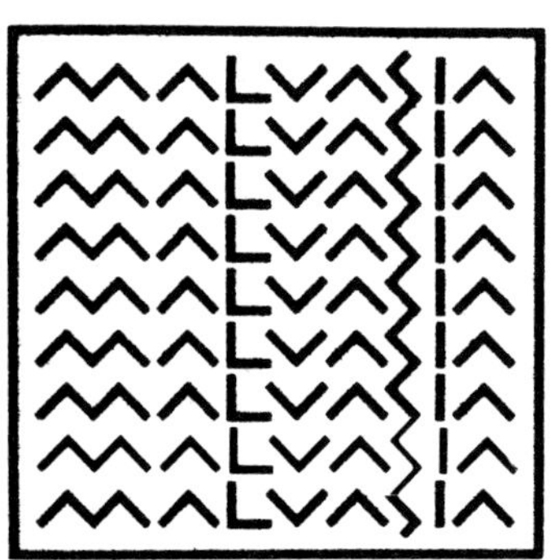

185 East 60th Street New York, N.Y. 10022
Phone/212-223-4790

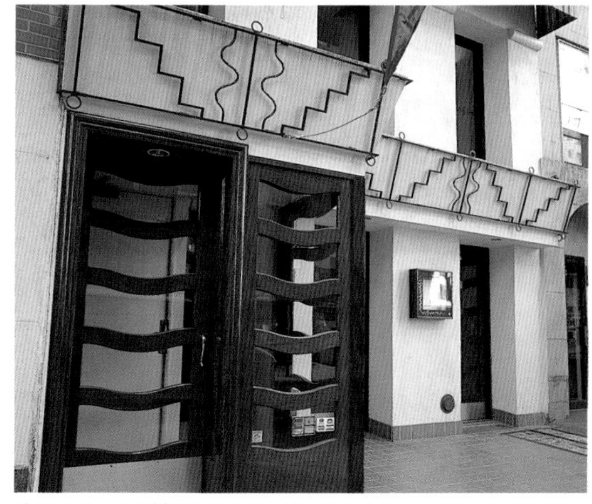

波のイメージを採り入れたファサード

The facade employing an image of waves.

入口近くに設けたバーコーナー　マホガニーとタイルを配したキュートな演出
The bar corner installed near the entrance; cutely presented with mahogany and tiles.

波のイメージの間接照明がある2階の客席
The 2nd floor guest seating area with indirect lighting which gives an image of waves.

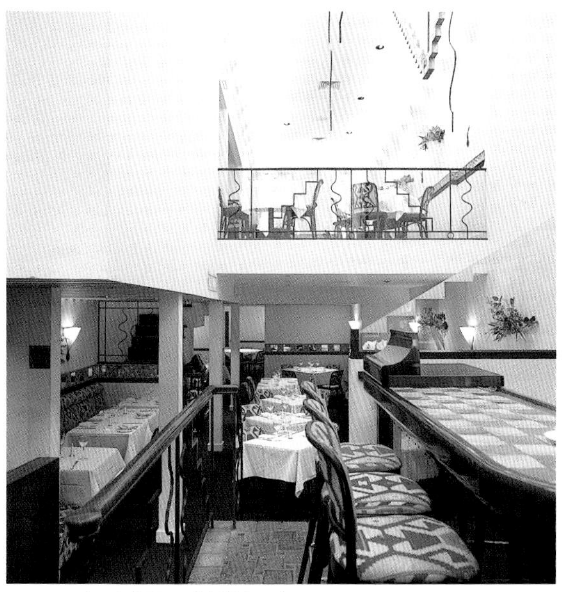

バーコーナーからテーブル席をみる
The table seating area viewed from the bar corner.

2階よりバーエリアを見おろす　テーマカラーはブルー　テラコッタ　ベージュなど
The bar area overlooked from the 2nd floor; the theme colors are blue, terra-cotta, beige, etc.

マルヴァシア
数多いマンハッタンのイタリア料理店の中で　今　最もホットなレストランのひとつで　店名はシェフでオーナーのジェナーロ　ピコネ(Gennaro Picone)氏の出身地　南イタリアのリパリ(Lipari)島のデザートワインに由来するという。デザインは「レミ(Remi)」本書P-83収録)のアダム　ティハニーで　リパリ島の家や　ギリシャ　アフリカ　イタリアなどのデザインを組み合わせた店づくりをしている。エレガントに仕上げられたスタッコの壁面に　夜の地中海の雰囲気をとり入れたり　波をイメージしたデザインが店の内外に見られる。
料理はイタリアと地中海料理がミックスされた独特なもので　シンプルだが強くコクのある味付けがモットー。客層はパーク　アヴェニュー(Park Avenue)のリッチな層が中心。

開店　　:1989年5月16日
営業時間:午前11時30分～午後3時(ランチ　月～土)
　　　　　午後6時～11時30分(ディナー)
客席数　:80席
従業員　:35名

MALVASIA

One of the most frequently cited restaurants among the many Italian restaurants in Manhattan, is "Malvasia" which has been named after a dessert wine produced in Lipari Island, South Italy, from which the chef-owner Gennaro Picone came. The design was undertaken by Adam D. Tihany who also designed "Remi" (see page 83), the restaurant design combines images of a house on Lipari Island with Greek, African and Italian images. The elegantly stuccoed wall introduces a nocturnal Mediterranean Sea mood, and both the interior and exterior are accented here and there with designs imitating waves.
The menu is comprised of unique foods cooked by mixing Italian and Mediterranean cuisine, and simply but savorily seasoned. It is frequented by rich customers on Park Avenue.

Opened　: May 16, 1989
Hours　: 11:30 a.m. to 3:00 p.m. (lunch – Monday to Saturday)
　　　6:00 p.m. to 11:30 p.m. (dinner)
Capacity　: 80 seats
Number of employees: 35

2nd plan

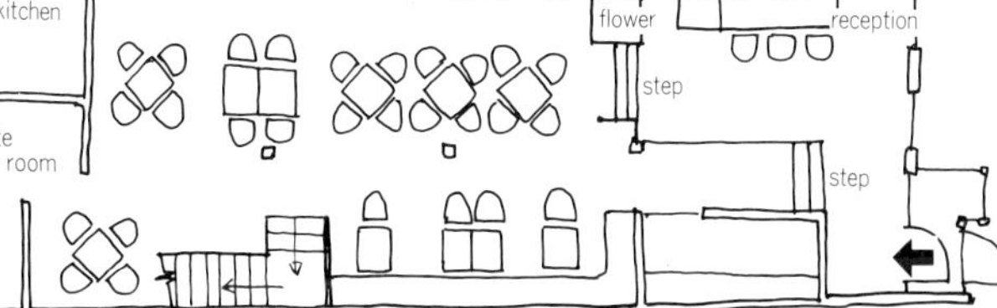

1st plan

1階客席(42席)の後方から入口方向を見る　ギリシャ アフリカ イタリアなどの文化をミックスした店内 の造り
The entrance area viewed from behind the 1st floor seating area (with 42 seats); the interior designed by mixing Greek, African, Italian and other cultural elements.

1/ PETTO DI ANITRA AL VINO DI MALVASIA CON DATTERI E OLIVE VERDI
Breast of Duck in MALVASIA Wine with Dates and Green Olives
2/ PASTA AND RISOTTO
3/ CASSATA SICILIANA
Sicilian Cheesecake
4/ INSALATA CALDA DI ARAGOSTA CON ARUGLA E AVOGATO
Warm Lobster Salad with Arugula and Avocado

盛り上った天井デザインの下に間接光が映し出すホワイトクロスのテーブルが連なる。連日 ファッショナブルな客たちで賑わう社交場でもある

Tables covered with a white cloth are arranged in a row receiving indirect light under the expansive ceiling design; "BICE" is also a social place crowded everyday with fashionable people.

7 East 54th Street New York, N.Y. 10022
Phone/212-688-1999

1926年創業の数字をきざむロゴが際立つファサード 店頭にはテラス席も並べられる

The facade with an impressive logo inscribed with "Founded in 1926"; the shop front is provided with a terrace seating area.

154席の店内で本場ミラノ料理がボリュームたっぷりにサービスされる。

In the 154-seated restaurant genuine Milano foods are served voluminously.

店内中央部の柱を利用したサービスステーション

The service station utilizing the central pillars.

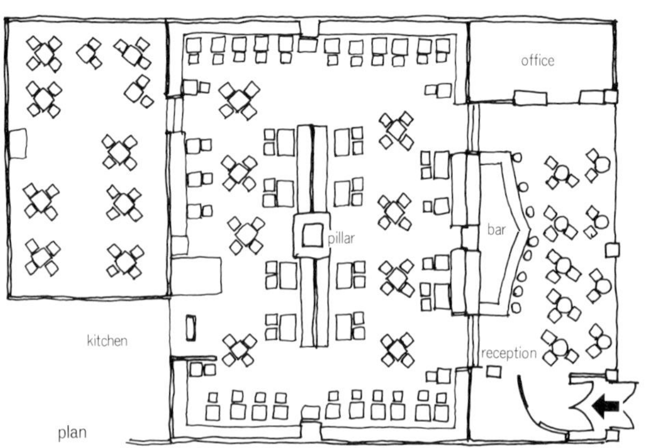

plan

ランチタイムには食事にも開放されるバーコーナー
At lunchtime the bar corner is opened to diners.

曲線を持たせたバーカウンター　右奥にダイニングエリアが見える
The curved bar counter and the dining corner on the inner right area.

ビーチェ

1926年にミラノにオープンした本格的な北イタリア料理店。パリに続きアメリカにも進出し人気は高い。1987年7月にニューヨーク店を開店して以来　ロサンゼルス　シカゴ　パームビーチ　ワシントンD.C.　アトランタなどに展開。以後マイアミ　そしてスペインのマドリッドにも開店の計画がある。

ニューヨーク店は　シェフをはじめスタッフはミラノの人が多く明るい。常にホットな話題を提供し　味　サービス　雰囲気ともに評論家の評価は高い。ほとんど柱を感じさせない広々とした154席の客席空間に　間接光に照らされたホワイトクロスのテーブルと　大きなウッドのチェアが連なる。デザインはアダム ティハニー（Adam D.Tihany)。昼はエグゼクティブやセクレタリィ　夜はドレスを着飾ったファッショナブルな客たちで賑わい　ニューヨークの社交レストランといった雰囲気。

開店　　：1987年7月7日
営業時間：正午～午後3時(ランチ　月～土)
　　　　午後6時～午前0時(ディナー　月～土　日曜は午後10時まで)
客席数　：154席　バー15席
従業員数：90名
客単価　：ランチ/40ドル　ディナー/60ドル

BICE

An orthodox Italian restaurant which opened in Milano in 1926, "Bice" has steadily developed its chain. After opening chain restaurants in Paris, it has also extended the chain across the U.S.A. Since opening in New York in July 1987, it has moved into Los Angeles, Chicago, Palm Beach, Washington D.C., Atlanta, etc. It is also planning to open in Miami and Madrid, Spain. Bice in New York has many Italian personnel, including the chef. Always offering up special dishes, it is highly rated by critics for its taste, service and atmosphere. On the 154-seat spacious guest area where one does not somehow feel the presence of pillars, white cloth tables and large wood chairs lie in rows under indirect lighting. The design is by Adam D. Tihany. In the daytime it is crowded with executives, secretaries, etc., while at night it is crowded with fashionably dressed guests. Thus, it has an atmosphere like a social restaurant in New York.

Opened : July 7, 1987
Hours : noon to 3:00 p.m.
(lunch – Monday to Saturday)
6:00 p.m. to 0:00 a.m.
(dinner – Monday to Saturday, till 10:00 p.m. on Sunday)
Capacity : 154 seats, bar 15 seats
Number of employees : 90
Price per customer : lunch/$40, dinner/$60

店内中央客席のユニークなデザインの椅子の仕切り

The central partition composed of uniquely designed chairs.

部屋のパーティションにしつらえた酒のボトルケース
The liquor bottle case installed at the room partition.

壁面の間接照明と背もたれのところに細長く配した鏡
The wall lighting for indirect light, and the slender mirror set on the chair's back.

①

③

②

④

1/ TORTELLONI DI VERZA, PATATE E PANCETTA AI PEPERONI DOLCI
Cabbage, potato and bacon ravioli with cream pepper sauce
2/ GAMBERONI HAWAIANI E CAPPESANTE CON RUCOLA
Hawaiian jumbo shrimp and scallops with arrugola
3/ SELLA DI CAPLIOLO ALLE BACCHE DI GINEPRO
Saddle of venison with juniper sauce
4/ TORTA ALL'ARANCIA GLASSATA AL CIOCCOLATO
Orange cake glazed with chocolate

左/従業員たちはイタリア人が多く サービスも明るく感じが良いのも評判だ

Left / Employees include many Italians whose cheerful and pleasant services are favorably reputed.

アート感覚あふれる1階のダイニングエリア

The 1st floor dining area full of artistic sense.

TRATTORIA DELL'ARTE

900 7th Avenue at 57th Street New York, N.Y. 10019
Phone/212-245-9800

イタリア人の大きな鼻をみせるファサードが目立つ
The facade impressive with an objet of Italian big nose.

カラフルで明るい店内ではファミリースタイルのイタリア料理を提供する

Family styled Italian foods are served in the bright, colorful restaurant.

くちびるの浮彫りも大胆にみせる壁面の演出
The wall presentation features the lips in bold relief.

グリーンの部屋からみたレストラン中央部の壁面
The wall in the center of the restaurant viewed from the green room.

トラットリア デルアルテ

店名は"美術のイタリアン レストラン"とうたった ミルトン グレイザー(Milton Glaser) 氏デザインの店。店内には人の耳 唇 乳房……など 体の一部を拡大した浮き彫りが壁面に飾られている。280席の広い店内は 1階にバーと3つのダイニングルームがあり 2階にはプライベート パーティに使用する部屋が用意されている。1階のバーに接するアンティパスト バーには常時20種類の冷製と温製のオードブルが用意されており ダイニングルームへ入る途中で客の目にとめさせるプレゼンテーションは たくみな演出だ。料理はこの他にピザ パスタや魚 仔牛肉の炭焼きなどで いずれもベーシックなイタリア料理を提供している。

開店　:1988年10月
営業時間:午前11時30分~午後3時(ランチ 月~金)
午前11時~午後4時(ランチ 土・日)
午後5時~午前0時(ディナー)
客席数 :280席
客単価 :ランチ/23ドル ディナー/30ドル

TRATTORIA DELL'ARTE

Designed by Milton Glaser, "Trattoria Dell'-Art" means an "Italian restaurant with fine arts." The interior features expanded body parts, such as ears, lips and breasts, in relief on the wall. The spacious interior has 280 seats, a bar and three dining rooms on the 1st floor, and rooms which can be used for private parties on the 2nd floor. An antipasto bar adjacent to another bar on the 1st floor always features 20 types of tastefully displayed cold and hot hors d'œuvre so that guests may be attracted to them before entering the dining rooms. Other menu items include pizza, pasta, fish, charcoal-cooked veal, etc. – basic Italian foods.

Opened : October 1988
Hours : 11:30 a.m. to 3:00 p.m. (lunch – Monday to Friday)
11:00 a.m. to 4:00 p.m. (lunch – Saturday and Sunday)
5:00 p.m. to 0:00 a.m. (dinner)
Capacity : 280 seats
Price per customer : lunch/$23, dinner/$30

ダ ヴィンチを想わせる人間のボディの部分スケッチで構成する壁面　空間デザイナーのミルトン グレイサー氏(Milton Glaser)が手掛けた話題のレストラン
The wall composed of partial sketches of human body which remind us of da Vinci; designed by Milton Glaser, space designer, "Trattoria Dell'Arte" is hotly talked about.

手前には人間の耳　後方にはくちびるの大きな浮彫りがみえる
Large ears in relief are visible on this side, while large lips in relief also stand out in bold relief behind.

乳房の下のテーブル席　ユーモアを感じさせる人気のあるコーナー
The table seating area under the breast; this corner is popular due to the humorous atmosphere.

常時20種類の料理が並べられているアンティパスト バー(Antipasto Bar)はバーコーナーに隣接している

20 types of dish are always displayed; an antipasto bar is adjacent to the bar corner.

ワイン テイスティングとプライベート ダイニングに使用される部屋

The room used for wine tasting and private dining.

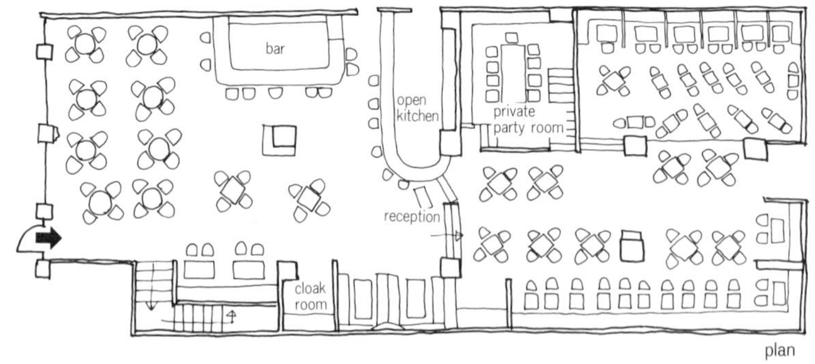

天井が高く明るい感じの店内

As one enters the restaurant, one feels a bright atmosphere under the high ceiling.

250 Park Avenue South New York, N.Y.
Phone/212-777-6211

パーク アベニューに面したファサード

The facade facing the park avenue.

125席の店内は中央にバーカウンターを配し　その廻りに段階的にテーブル席が展開する

The interior with 125 seats has a bar counter in the center around which the table seating area is arranged in tiers.

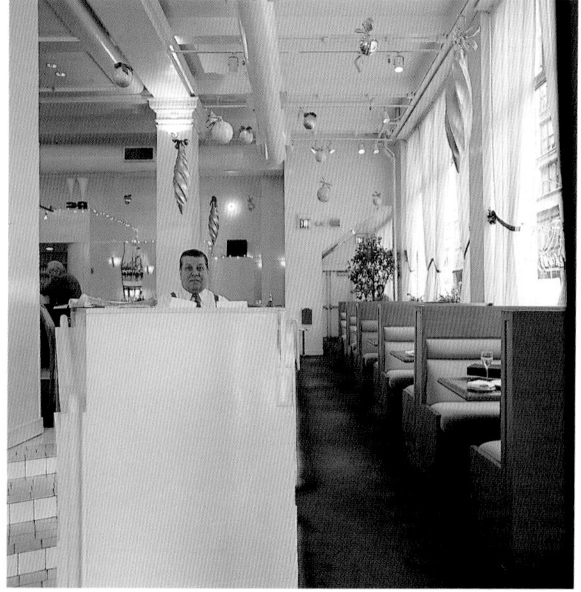

レセプションと窓際のブース席をみる

The reception and booth seating area by the window.

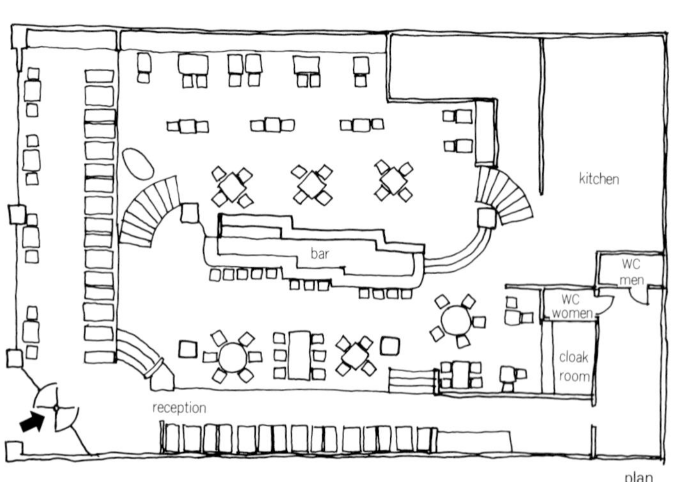

plan

手前の変形バーカウンターとエントランス方向をみる
The deformed bar counter on this side, and the entrance area.

ワインの販促にも力を入れ　一人客には食事用に開放するバーコーナー
Wine sales promotion is also active, and the bar corner is also opened to those who come to dine alone.

ポジタノ

イタリアのアマルフィ(Amalfi)海岸沿いのナポリとサレルノ(Salerno)の中間に位置する　ロマンティックで歴史を持つ町ポジタノ(Positano)が店名の由来。この地方は　シーフードやパスタをはじめ比較的軽い料理が多い所だ。この町で生まれ育ったルイジ　セレンタノ(Luigi Celentano)氏を開店と同時にシェフに迎え　ニューヨークのイタリアン　レストランの中で確固たる地位を保っている。2階建ての店内は　天井が高く　広々とした空間に段階的なテーブルで構成し　その中間部にバーエリアを設けている。手入れの行き届いた居心地のよい店内は好評で　アメリカ人たちはロマンティックなレストランと表現している。周囲の広告会社の社員やクライアントたちを中心に賑わっている。また一人客にはバーカウンターを食事用に開放しているのも好評。

開店　：1984年12月18日
営業時間：正午～午後3時(ランチ　月～金)
午後5時30分～午後11時30分(ディナー　月～木/金・土は午前0時30分まで)
客席数　：125席　バー12席
従業員数：50名
客単価　：ランチ/30ドル　ディナー/40ドル

POSITANO

The restaurant was named after Positano, a romantic and historic town situated between Naples and Salerno near Amalfi, Italy. Food in the town is relatively light, composed of seafood and pasta. When "Positano" opened, Luigi Celentano, who was born and brought up in the town, was invited in as a chef, and it has thereafter maintained a firm position among Italian restaurants in New York. The interior utilizes a wide space under a high ceiling in a two-storied building, with tables gradually arranged on different levels. In the center is a bar area. The neatly arranged comfortable interior is favorably accepted by Americans who feel that "Positano" is a romantic restaurant. It is crowded primarily with workers and clients of neighboring advertising companies. The bar is open to all those who come alone – another popular feature of the restaurant.

Opened : December 18, 1984
Hours : noon to 3:00 p.m.
(lunch – Monday to Friday)
5:30 p.m. to 11:30 p.m.
(dinner – Monday to Thursday, till 0:30 a.m. on Friday and Saturday)
Capacity : 125 seats, bar 12 seats
Number of employees: 50
Price per customer : lunch/$30, dinner/$40

店内を俯瞰する　居ここちが良くロマンチックな造りと好評

Overlooking the interior; favorably accepted as being comfortable and romantic.

最上部にあるテーブル席 ミラーを使った壁面構成で店内を広くみせる

The table seating area at the uppermost level; the interior designed to give a spacious impression by means of the mirror-finished wall.

コーナーに設けたサービス ステーション

The service station installed on the corner.

左/オープン以来確固たる評判の料理を提供するシェフ・Luigi Celentano氏

Left / The chef Luigi Celentano who has continued to offer highly reputed dishes since the opening.

1/ LINGUINE ALLE COZZE
Linguine with Squid, Garlic, Olive Oil and Tomato
2/ GAMBERONI ALLA SALENTINA
Jumbo Shrimp sauteed with Scallions, served with Black Beans and Rice.
3/ PETTO DI POLLO OLTA MEDITERRANEA
Chicken breast on Red Pepper Sauce with Avocado and Rice.
4/ MEDOGLIONI DI CERVO ALLE ERBE
Medallions of roasted venison with polenta

①

③

②

④

通りに面したダイニングエリア　円柱があり地中海地方の遺跡を思わせる

As one enters the restaurant, one feels an atmosphere which reminds us of the Mediterranean remains; the dining area facing the reception and colonnaded street.

SFUZZI

53 West 65th Street New York, N.Y. 10023
Phone/212-873-3700

右/リンカーンセンターにも近い好立地で　カラフルなファサードが目立つ

Right / Favorably situated near the Lincoln Center, the "SFUZZI" stands out with the colorful facade.

柱や壁面の一部が崩れ落ちた　廃墟の中のレストランのイメージを演出している

Presents an image of restaurant in the midst of ruins, with its pillars and walls partially collapsed.

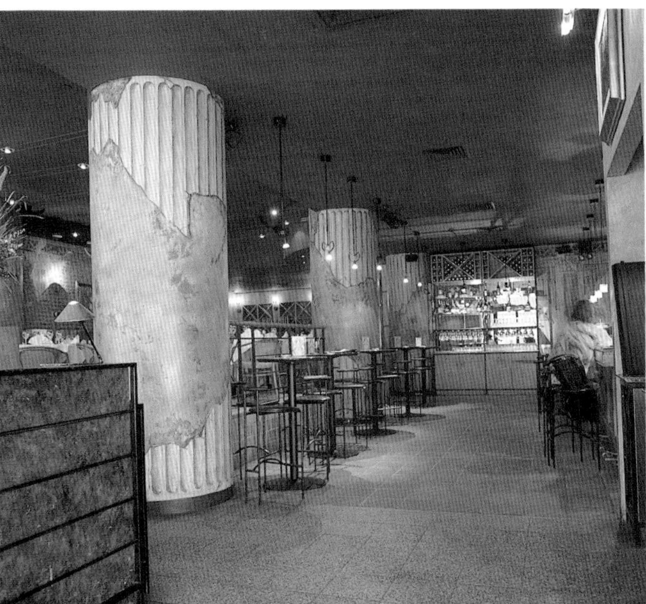

上/石材とアイアン フレームのレセプション 廻りの雰囲気に溶け込んでいる
中/レセプションの右側にあるバーエリア
下/コーナーを利用した三角形のテーブル席

Top / The reception built by using stone and iron framing; fuses into the surrounding atmosphere.
Center / The bar area installed on the right side of the reception.
Bottom / The triangular table seating area utilizing a corner.

フージ

1987年に第1号店をダラスに開店し アップスケールなイタリアン レストランとして注目されている。現在ヒューストン ニューヨーク ワシントンD.C. ボストン フィラデルフィア デンバーなどに急速な展開を進めている。店名はイタリア語のスラングで"楽しい料理"という意味。デザインは地中海地方の遺跡をテーマにしている。メニューは前菜が9種 ピザが5種 パスタが6種 魚 チキン 肉料理などのスペシャリティが7種 サイドオーダーが4種などで構成され 価格は4～25ドルである。スペシャリティはユニフォームメニューを採用し どの店へ行っても同じクォリティで同じ味の料理が食べられるというのが特徴。特にソース類は営業の直前に作り新鮮さを重視するなど 手作り感をアピールしている。

開店　　:1988年5月
営業時間:午前11時30分～午後3時(ランチ)
　　　　　午後5時～午後11時30分(ディナー)
客席数　:160席
従業員数:85名
客単価　:ランチ/20ドル　ディナー/30ドル

SFUZZI

Since the first restaurant opened in 1987 in Dallas, "Sfuzzi" has drawn attention as an upscale Italian restaurant chain. At present, the chain is rapidly developing in Houston, New York, Washington D.C., Boston, Philadelphia, Denver, etc.
The name means "enjoyable dishes" in Italian slang, and the design incorporates imitations of historical remains found in the Mediterranean. The menu features 9 types of hors d'œuvre, 5 types of pizza, 6 types of pasta, and 7 types of fish, chicken and meat spécialité.
Side orders for 4 types of meals are also accepted for $4 to $25. Since the chain employs a uniform spécialité menu, customers can find the same quality at any of their restaurants. Sauces, like other ingredients, are prepared just before they are served ensuring freshness, thereby stressing the chain's ambience of handmade foods.

Opened : May 1988
Hours : 11:30 a.m. to 3:00 p.m. (lunch)
5:00 p.m. to 11:30 p.m. (dinner)
Capacity : 160 seats
Number of employees: 85
Price per customer : lunch/$20, dinner/$30

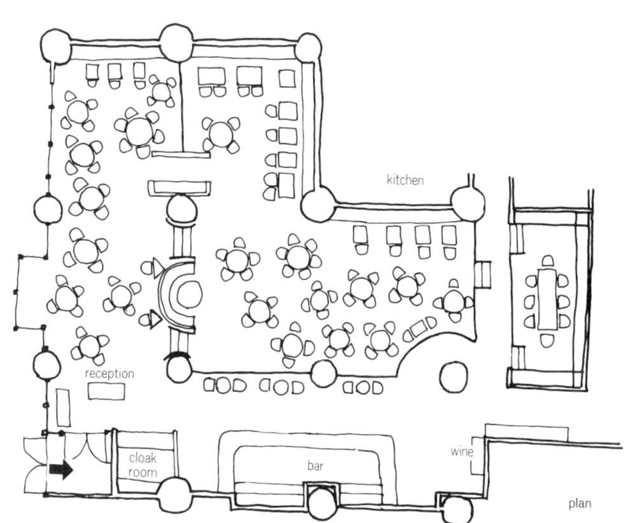

円柱やレンガの壁の中に一際目立つ中央の白いテーブル席　後方にはグループ客用の席があり　ワインセラーを設けたコーナーがみえる
The white table seating area which stands out vividly against the columns and bricked wall; behind the table is visible a wine cellar corner which is also provided with seats for group guests.

一段高いテーブル席からバーコーナーを見下ろす
The bar corner overlooked from the table seating area which is higher than the surrounding floor.

フルーツや香草を使用したファッションドリンクスも人気がある　TVモニターの設置も欠かせないバーコーナー
Fashion drinks using fruits or herb are also popular; the bar corner equipped with TV monitors as indispensable equipment.

店内奥よりダイニングエリアとバーコーナーをみる

The dining area and bar corner viewed from an inner part.

Fresh Mozzarella with Roma Tomatoes Roasted Peppers and Basil Pesto

Grilled Vegetables with Balsamic Vinegar and Extra Virgin Olive Oil.

アッパー イーストサイドの高級住宅と高級ショップがまわりにある好立地で 店名の表示を小さくしたファサード

Favorably situated in an area surrounded with high class residences and shops on the Upper East Side, the facade bears a small logo of the restaurant name.

Coco Pazzo

23 East 74th Street New York, N. Y. 10021
Phone/212-794-0205

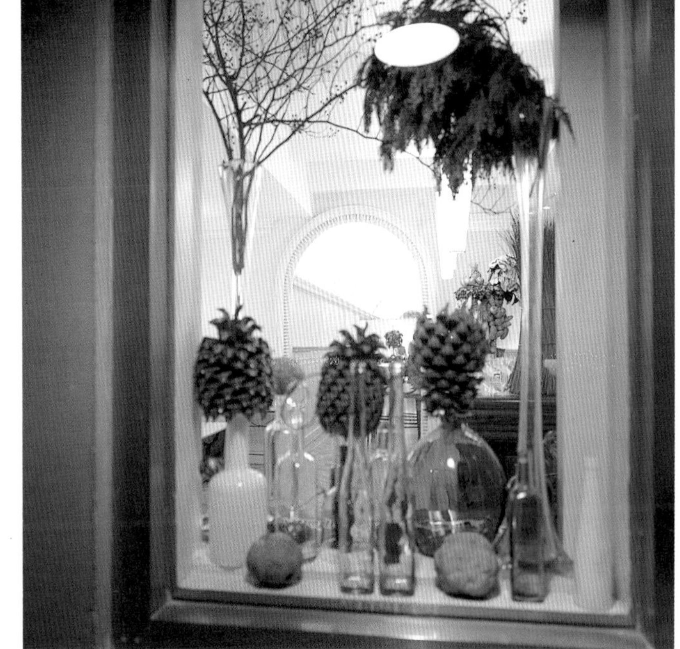

店内をそれとなく見せる小窓とそのディスプレイ

The small window designed to allow a casual glance at the interior, and its display.

入口近くのバーコーナーから円形天井の通路と奥のダイニングルームをみる

The aisle under the roundish ceiling and inner dining room viewed from the bar corner near the entrance.

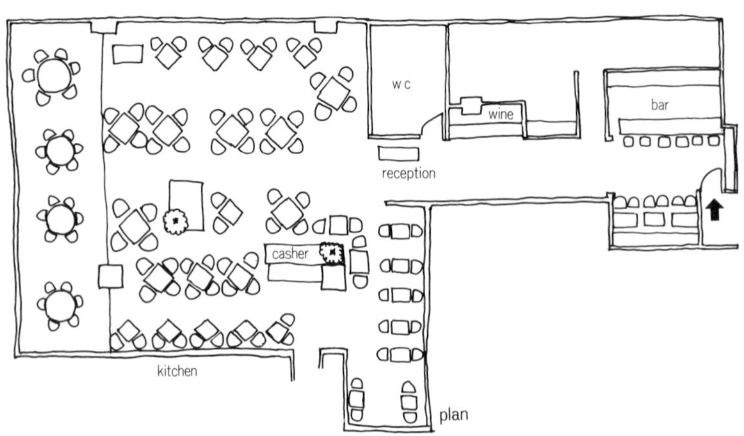

小スペースのバーコーナー

The bar corner with a small space.

デコレーションにも気を配るバーコーナー

The bar corner which is carefully decorated.

ココ パッヅォ

ニューヨークの高級イタリアンレストラン「ル マドリ(Le Madri)」のオーナー ピノ ルオンゴ(Pino Luongo)氏が 高級ブティック「バーニーズ(Barney's)」のプレスマン ファミリーと組んで出店したイタリア料理店。客単価はランチ20ドル ディナー30ドルと「マドリ」の約半分である。店名は英語で"クレイジー シェフ"という意味。料理はアペタイザーやパスタ料理に力を入れ 週末にはグループ客をターゲットに 大皿に盛りつけたファミリースタイルのサービスを提供している。最近のアメリカにおける傾向として 高級レストランよりも このクラスのレストランの需要が高くなってきており 新たな出店や既存店においても価格の見直しがなされている。

開店 :1990年11月27日
営業時間:正午～午後3時(ランチ)
午後6時～午前0時(ディナー)
客席数 :100席 バー12席
従業員数:40名
客単価 :ランチ/20ドル ディナー/30ドル

COCO PAZZO

This Italian restaurant was opened by Pino Luongo, owner of "Le Madri," a high class Italian restaurant in New York, together with the Pressman Family which owns the high class boutique "Barney's." The average price per customer is $20 for lunch and $30 for dinner – about half those at "Madri." The restaurant name means a "crazy chef" in English. The menu an particular features appetizers and pastas, and on the weekend a family style large plate service intended for group customers is offered. One of the contemporary tendencies in America is that demand for this level of restaurant – not high class restaurants – is growing, and newly opened and existing restaurants are being forced to revise their prices.

Opened : November 27, 1990
Hours : noon to 3:00 p.m. (lunch)
6:00 p.m. to 0:00 a.m. (dinner)
Capacity : 100 seats, bar 12 seats
Number of employees: 40
Price per customer : lunch/$20,
dinner/$30

ウッドパネルの重厚なワインセラーを設けた通路

The aisle provided with a dignified wood-panelled wine cellar.

ダイニングルーム　入口際のハムやチーズのディスプレイと清潔でカジュアルな雰囲気の客席
The display of ham, cheese, etc. by the entrance to the dining room, and the guest seating area in a clean and casual atmosphere.

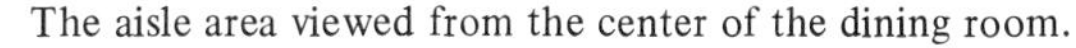

ダイニングルームの中央部から通路方向をみる
The aisle area viewed from the center of the dining room.

壁面を構成する大きなミラーやフラスコ画
The large mirror and fresco which compose the wall.

ダイニングルームの中央に置かれたアンティパストのテーブルとオーナーのPino Luongo氏とシェフのMark Strausman氏
The antipasto table installed in the center of the dining room, and the owner Pino Luongo and the chef Mark Strausman.

①

②

③

1/ Roasted Snapper/Rosemary and Lemon
2/ Stuffed Breast of Pheasant and Tuscan Liver and Mushroom Pate
3/ Baked Pear in Red Wine

店内奥から入口とバー方向をみる　45席という小じんまりとした客席にはアンティパストのディスプレイを設けている
The entrance and bar area viewed from an inner part; the cozy guest area with only 45 seats is provided with an antipasto display.

RISTORANTE daUMBERTO

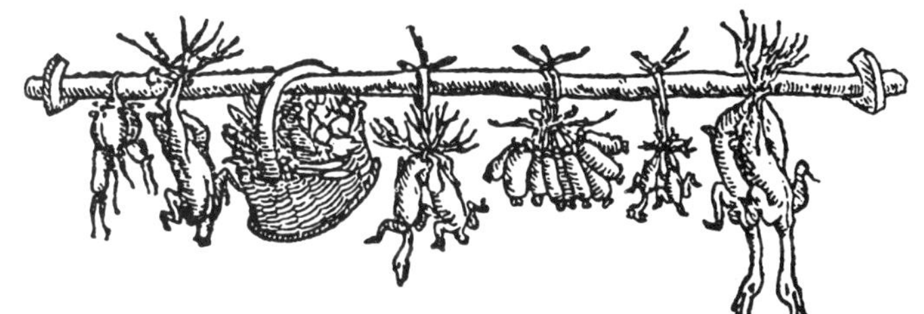

107 West 17th Street New York, N. Y. 10011
Phone/212-989-0303

朱色で目立つファサード　The vermilion facade stands out.

イエローの壁面　木のフロアなど　アットホームな温かい雰囲気のダイニングルーム
The dining room has a homely and warm atmosphere with the yellow wall, wooden floor, etc.

ダ ウンベルト

6番街(Sixth Avenue)と7番街(Seventh Avenue)の中間のチェルシー(Chersy)地区に位置するイタリアン レストラン。フローレンス地方の料理がメインで　特にシェフでオーナーのウンベルト アサンテ(Umberto Assante)氏がつくる20～25種のアンティパスト料理が好評。温かいイエローの壁に囲まれ　45席とこじんまりしている店内は　混雑してくると　少少騒々しく熱狂的な感さえするが　フロントの息子のヴィットリオ(Vittorio)氏やスタッフの親しみのあるサービスやきびきびした動きなどが気持よく　明るい雰囲気があたかもイタリアにいるような錯覚をあたえる。

開　　店:1987年11月15日
営業時間:正午～午後3時(ランチ 月～金)
　　　　午後5時30分～11時(ディナー 月～木 金・土は11時30分まで)
客 席 数:45席
従業員数:27名
客 単 価:45ドル

DA UMBERTO

An Italian restaurant situated in the Chersy area between Sixth Avenue and Seventh Avenue. Mainly serving Florentine foods, "Da Umberto" specifically features 20 to 25 types of antipasto cooked by the chef and owner Umberto Assante. Surrounded with warm yellow walls, the interior space has 45 neatly installed seats. When it gets congested, it becomes a little noisy and hectic. However, due to the hospitable service and quick response of Mr. Vittorio, son of the owner, who sits by the front desk, and staff, one feels pleasant in a bright atmosphere – as if one was in Italy.

Opened : November 15, 1987
Hours : noon to 3:00 p,m. (lunch – Monday to Friday)
5:30 p.m. to 11:00 p.m. (dinner – Monday to Thursday, till 11:30 p.m. on Friday and Saturday)
Capacity : 45 seats
Number of employees: 27
Price per customer : $45

壁面と天井に向けた間接照明をアクセントにしたダイニングルームをみる　奥には自然光を採り入れた客席もある

The dining room accented with indirect lighting which is directed towards the wall and ceiling; on an inner part there is a guest seating area which is designed to let in natural light.

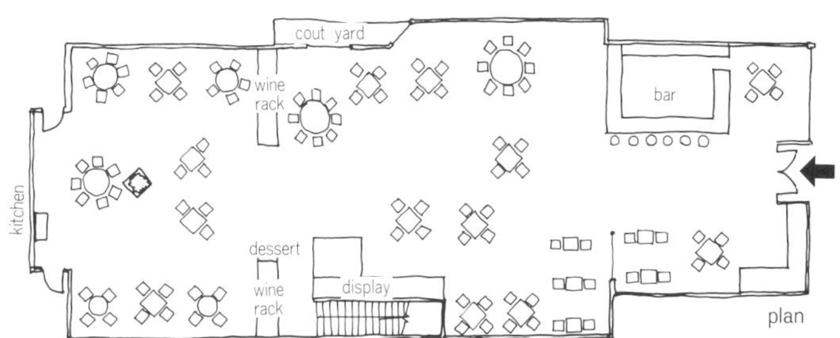

入口近くのバーコーナー

The bar corner installed near the entrance.

ダイニングルームのアンティパストのディスプレイ

The antipasto display installed in the dining room.

毎日20～25種のアンティパストを揃えている　またイタリアン ワインのコレクションも豊富だ
20 to 25 types of antipasto are prepared everyday; a rich collection of Italian wine is also displayed.

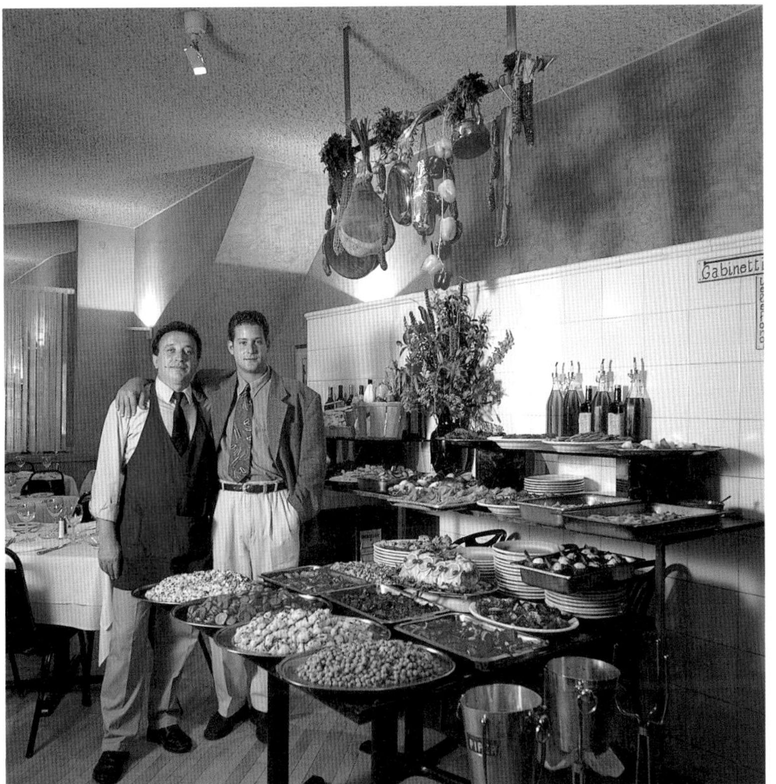

フロントの総指揮者であるオーナーの Vittorio 氏と右腕で キャプテンの Gianny M 氏
The owner Vittorio who generally superintends the front, and his right arm and captain Gianny M.

上/天窓のある奥のダイニングルームとオープンキッチン
下/客席の様子をみながら料理が作れるというシェフ＆オーナーのUmberto氏も自慢のオープンキッチン

Top / The inner dining room and open kitchen provided with a skylight.
Bottom / The open kitchen with which the chef & owner Umberto is satisfied, since he can cook while viewing the guest seating area.

ダークウッドのパネル　絵画　大理石のフロアで構成する格調あるエントランス付近からダイニングルーム方向をみる
The dining room area viewed from the dignified entrance area which is composed of dark wood panels, paintings and marble floor.

Mondrian

7 East 59th Street New York, N. Y. 10022
Phone/212-935-3434

金色を配したファサード　The facade accented with gold.

格調あるダイニングルーム　大きな飾り皿を中心にエレガントなテーブル セッティングがされている

The dignified dining room is provided with elegant table setting, centering around a large decoration plate.

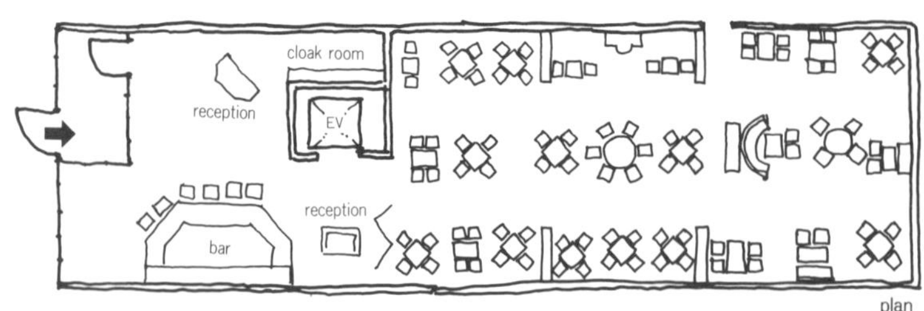

調度品のようなサービス ステーション

The service station which looks like a set of fixtures.

壁面にはホアン ミロ ランディ ホワイト ヘンリィ ムーア等の作品が飾られ まるで美術館にいるような雰囲気
The wall is decorated with paintings of Joan Miró, Randy White, Henry Moore, etc., so that one feels as if one sits in an art gallery.

ダイニングエリアから入口近くのバーエリアをみる
The bar area near the entrance viewed from the dining area.

モンドリアン

「モンドリアン」は アーティスティックなインテリアと 素材や盛りつけのハーモニーを強調した料理 そして素晴らしいサービスで多くの客をつかんでいる。店名はフランスのアブストラクト画家のピエット モンドリアンに由来する。インテリアはフィリップ ジョージ (Philip George)のデザイン。壁画にはヘンリー ムーア ホアン ミロ ランディ ホワイトなどの絵画が飾られている。料理は いまニューヨークを代表するシェフの一人若手のトーマス コリッチオ(Thomas Colicchio)で 素材を重要視し それらの味のハーモニーを立体的な盛りつけに仕上げた新しいスタイルのもの。

開店　：1988年9月
営業時間：正午～午後2時30分(月～金 ランチ)
午後5時30分～10時30分(月～土 ディナー)
客席数　：96席　個室25席
従業員数：30名

MONDRIAN

"Mondrian" intrigues many customers with its artistic interior, and with its dishes cooked by stressing a harmony of materials and arrangements, and wonderful service. The shop name comes from Piet Mondrian, a French abstract painter. The walls are decorated with the paintings of Henry Moore, Joan Miró, Randy White, etc. The food is cooked by Thomas Colicchio, a young representative New York chef, who makes much of materials and assortments by harmonizing tastes in a cubic style.

Opened : September 1988
Hours : noon to 2:30 p.m.
(lunch – Monday to Friday)
5:30 p.m. to 10:30 p.m.
(dinner – Monday to Saturday)
Capacity : 96 seats, private room 25 seats
Number of employees : 30

上/地階にあるプライベート ダイニングルーム(25席)はよりコンテンポラリィな雰囲気で ワインセラーも備えている
下/現代のN.Y.を代表するシェフの一人として注目されているThomas Colicchio氏は29才の若さである

Top / The private dining room (with 25 seats) in the basement has a more contemporary atmosphere and is also provided with a wine cellar.
Bottom / Thomas Colicchio, who is drawing attention as one of representative contemporary chefs in New York, is only 29 years old.

①

③

④

②

1/ Crab and Ssparagus Salad with Celery Chips and Curry oil.
2/ Tuna and Salmon Tartare with Sea Urchin Vinaigrette.
3/ Blackberry Meringue with Roasted Pears.
4/ Lace Cookies with Sweet Goat Cheese and Raspberries.

高級住宅が多いアッパー イースト サイドのタウンハウスを改装したファサード

The facade made by renewing a town house on the Upper East Side where there are many gorgeous residences.

AUREOLE

34 East 61st Street New York, N.Y. 10021
Phone/212-319-1660

2階　曲線の手摺りと大きなピッチャーウインドがあるテーブル席

The 2nd floor table seating area with the curved handrails and large pitcher window.

2階からエントランス方向を俯瞰する　壁面には鳥を表現したプラスターのレリーフがある
The entrance area overlooked from the 2nd floor; accented with plastered birds in relief on the wall.

大きな生花をアクセントにした1階のダイニングルーム　壁面のレリーフには動物や魚の姿を浮き出させている
The 1st floor dining room accented with large flower arrangements; animals and fish expressed in relief on the wall.

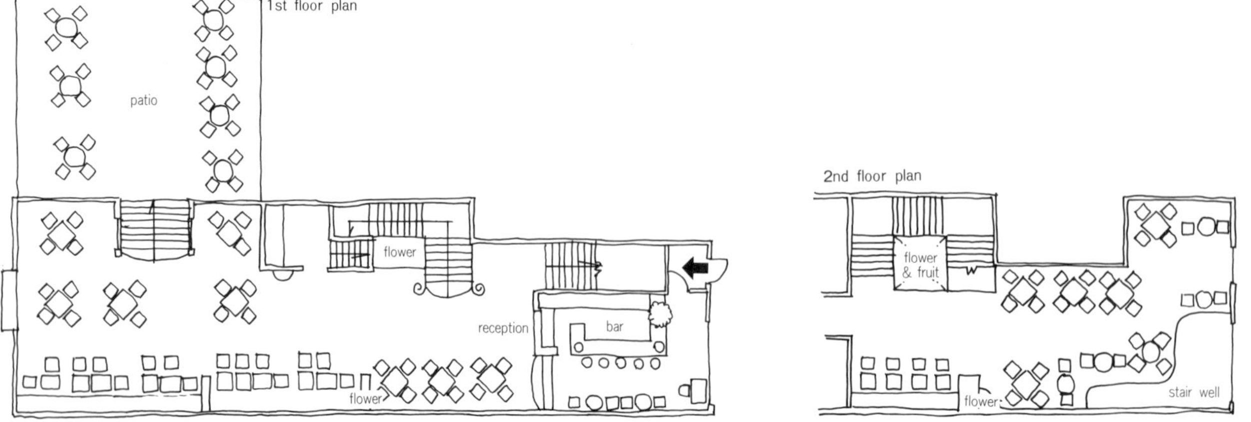

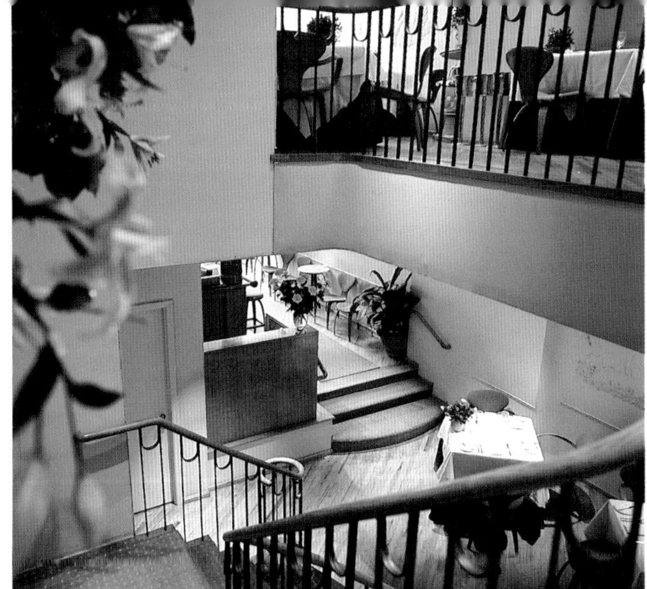

上/階段の中程より 1階のレセプションあたりと2階のテーブル席をみる
下/2階ダイニングエリアに通じる重厚な感じのステアーウェイ

Top / The 1st floor reception area and the 2nd floor table seating area viewed from the middle of the staircase.
Bottom / The dignified stairway leading to the dining area on the 2nd floor.

有名人の利用も多く　かなり以前から予約が必要なN.Y.の高級レストランの1つ　男性はネクタイ着用

Visited by many celebrated people, "AUREOLE" is one of high-class restaurants in New York which needs reservation considerably beforehand; male guests must wear a tie.

入口際のバーコーナー　上部は吹抜けになっている

The bar corner near the entrance; a stairwell is secured on the upper part.

オーリオーレ

90年代のアメリカ料理界をリードする料理人の一人として注目されているのが　このレストランのオーナー シェフ　チャーリー パーマー(Charlie Palmer)氏。80年代のヘルシーブームで　クリームやコレステロールや脂肪分を配慮したメニューが一般的になったが　彼の料理にはこのこだわりがなく　それぞれの長所を取り入れ　季節の新鮮な食材を活かし　うまい料理を創り出すことに特徴がある。さらに舌ざわりや盛り付けの美しさなどが加わったイノベイティブ クイジーンで開店以来盛況　特にプリフィックス ディナーに人気があり　シェフの自慢料理が楽しめ　有名人の利用も多い。高級住宅が多いアッパー イースト サイド(Upper East Side)のタウンハウスの1・2階に位置し　店頭には2階まである大きな窓ガラスが配され　クリームトーンの壁にはプラスターのレリーフが　蛙　鹿　ジャンプする魚や鳥たちなどの姿を浮き出させているのが印象的。大きな生け花がところどころにアクセントとして置かれているのもこのレストランのイメージにマッチしている。

開店:1988年11月4日

営業時間:正午～午後2時30分(ランチ　月～土)
午後6時～10時30分(ディナー　月～木)
午後5時30分～11時(ディナー　金・土)

客 席 数:95席

従業員数:75名

客 単 位:ランチ/30ドル　ディナー/65ドル

AUREOLE

The restaurant's owner-chef Charlie Palmer is drawing attention as one of the cooks leading the American cooking business in the 1990s. Reflecting the health food boom in the 1980s, menus with moderate quantities of cream, cholesterol and fat have become popular. However, Palmer's foods are cooked without taking particular care about these ingredients, but are characterized by the adherence to "good taste" realized by utilizing fresh seasonal materials while taking account of their respective features regarding their ingredients, etc. Coupled with the feel on the tongue and the beautiful arrangements, his dishes have been favorably accepted as an innovative cuisine since the restaurant was opened. Prefixed dinners, among other types, are very popular, since the chef's proud foods can be enjoyed. Thus, "Aureole" is also frequented by celebrated guests. Situated on the 1st and 2nd floors of a town house on the Upper East Side where there are many deluxe residences, the restaurant features a large shop-front glass window which covers even the front face of the 2nd floor. The cream-toned wall is decorated with impressive reliefs of frogs, deer, jumping fish, birds, etc. on the plaster. Large flowers arranged here and there as an accent match the restaurant's image.

Opened : November 4, 1988

Hours : noon to 2:30 p.m. (lunch – Monday to Saturday)
6:00 p.m. to 10:30 p.m. (dinner – Monday to Thursday)
5:30 p.m. to 11:00 p.m. (dinner – Friday and Saturday)

Capacity : 95 seats

Number of employees: 75

Price per customer : lunch/$30, dinner/$65

90年代のアメリカ料理界をリードする一人としてイノベイティブ クイジーンを提供するオーナー シェフのCharlie Palmer氏

One of chefs leading the American cuisine circle in the 1990s, the owner-chef Charlie Palmer offers innovative cuisine.

①

②

③

1/ Terrine of Root Vegetables with Warm Grilled Endive
charred tomato vinaigrette, crisped carrot.
2/ Cool Poached Lobster Salad with New Potatoes
lemon essence, mesclun greens and basil cream.
3/ Oak Smoked Salmon with Cucumber Salad
double cultured cream and Michael's sourdough toasts.

入口際のテーブル席からレセプションと2階の客席をみる　壁面はアボカド グリーンとパパイヤ ゴールド

The reception and the 2nd floor guest seating area viewed from the table seating area by the entrance; the wall is finished in avocado green and papaya gold.

MESA

GRILL

102 Fifth Avenue New York, N.Y. 10011
Phone/212-807-7400

フラットアイアン地区のビルを改装し　話題となったファサード

The topical facade made by redecorating a building on the Flatiron District.

客席奥からバーエリア方向をみる　中央には4本の太いコンクリートの柱が並んでいる
The bar area viewed from the inner guest seating area; in the center four thick concrete pillars stand in a row.

高い空間に変化をつけたレイアウトとカラフルで遊び心を配したカジュアルなインテリア
The layout over a high space with varied expressions, and the colorful and casual interior designed with a playful spirit.

メサ グリル

80年代に入って注目され始めてきた5番街(Fifth Avenue)の南 フラットアイアン地区には 広告代理店や有名出版社 芸術家たちのスタジオが集まっており活況を呈している。「メサ グリル」はそんな場所に立地している。サウス ウエスタン スタイルのこのレストランは 「ゴッサム バー&グリル(Gotham Bar & Grill)」のオーナーで 不動産デベロッパーのジェリー クレッチマー(Jerry Kretchmer)氏とジェフ ブリス(Jeff Bliss)氏の経営。シェフには若いボビー フレイ(Bobby Flay)を迎え サウスウエスタンのメキシコ調に よりアメリカン スタイルを加え アップグレードさせた料理を提供している。店内はジェイムス ビバー(James Biber)氏のカラフルで 遊び心を配したカジュアルなインテリア。いずれも話題になり好評である。

開店 店:1991年1月15日
営業時間:正午~午後2時(ランチ 月~金)
午後5時30分~10時30分(ディナー)
客 席 数:135席 バーカウンター 16席
従業員数:60名
客 単 価:ランチ/22ドル ディナー/35ドル(いずれも飲物別)

MESA GRILL

The Flatiron area south of Fifth Avenue began to draw attention in the 1980s, and an increasing number of advertising agents, famous publishers and artists' studios have gathered here, creating a brisk atmosphere. The "Mesa Grill" is situated in such an environment. The restaurant is in the Southwestern style and is managed by Jerry Kretchmer, owner of "Gotham Bar & Grill" and real estate developer, and Jeff Bliss. Bobby Flay, a young chef invited in by them, serves upgraded Southwestern Mexican foods accented with a more American style. The interior has drawn attention due to the colorful and casual interior with the spirit of play designed by James Biber.

Opened : January 15, 1991
Hours : noon to 2:00 p.m. (lunch – Monday to Friday)
5:30 p.m. to 10:30 p.m. (dinner)
Capacity : 135 seats, bar counter 16 seats
Number of employees: 60
Price per customer : lunch/$22, dinner/$35 (excluding drinks)

2階よりバーを中心に俯瞰する　小さな穴のあるアルミニュームの照明やワイヤーを使用したファンも特製

The interior centering around the bar overlooked from the 2nd floor; with specially designed lighting equipment finished with aluminum having small holes, and fans using wires.

サウスウエスタン調のカラーを配したバーコーナー　The bar corner decorated with Southwestern colors.

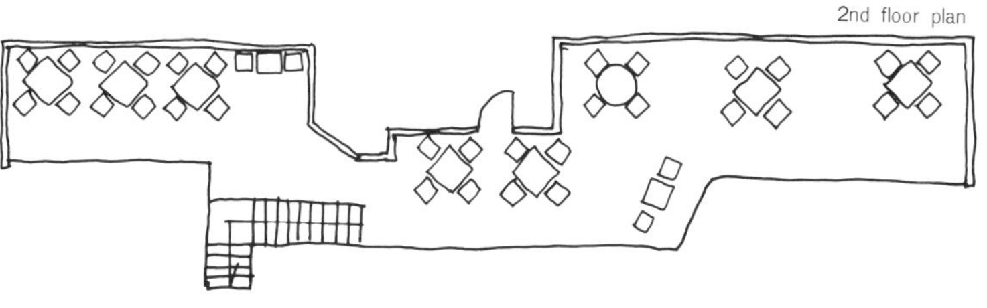

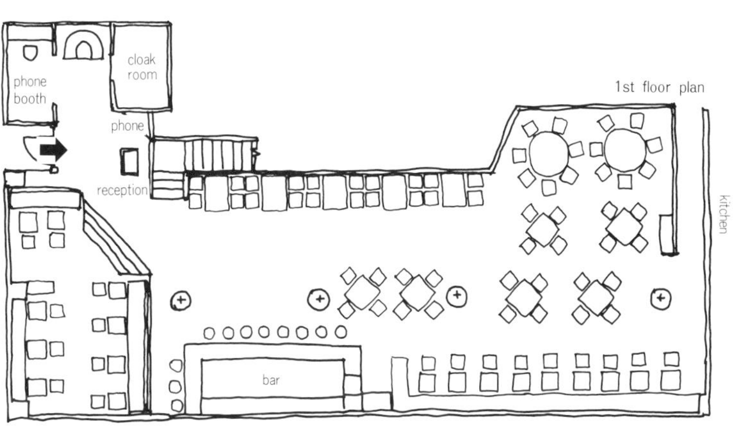

イエローキャブの椅子があるテーブル席　奥にはオープンキッチンがみえる
The table seating area equipped with yellow-capped chairs; the open kitchen is visible behind.

2階の客席
The 2nd floor guest seating area.

入口際より奥行きのある客席をみる　手前の長椅子にはカウボーイをテーマにした柄がプリントされている
The guest seating area having a large depth, as viewed from the entrance; the sofa on this side features printed patterns of cowboy.

①

③

②

26才のN.Y.生まれのシェフ・Bobby Flay氏のサウスウエスタンに よりアメリカンスタイルを加え グレードアップさせた料理

1/ Grilled Tuna Tostada
with Black Bean-Mango Salsa + Avocado Vinaigrette.
2/ Tomato Tortilla Soup
garnished with Avocado, White Cheddar Cheese + Cilantro.
3/ New Mexican Style Barbequed Salmon
served with Southwestern Potato Salad + Chipotle Corn on the Cob.

エントランス ホールからレセプションをみる　深海色のアース カラー(Crimson-earth)の壁面や自然木を使用し　スペインのカタロニア地方の雰囲気を出している
The reception viewed from the entrance hall; by using crimson-earth colored wall and natural wood, the interior creates an atmosphere of Catalonia, Spain.

47-49 West 55 Street New York, N. Y. 10019
Phone/212-586-3434

ファサード　The facade.

カウンターのデザインがユニークなバーコーナー

The bar corner whose counter is uniquely designed.

自然木のカウンターバー

The counter bar finished with natural wood.

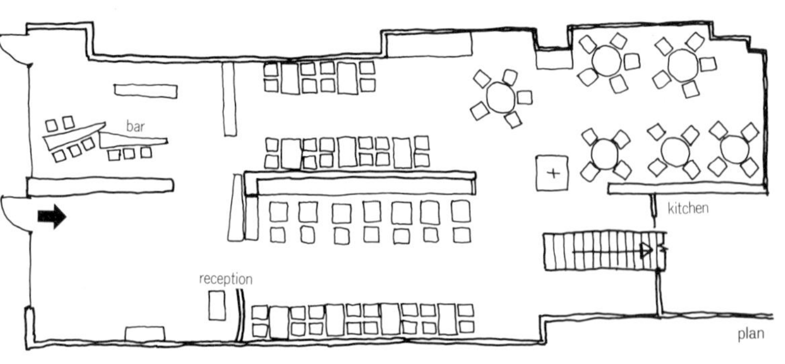

1階のダイニングルーム　オニキスの照明器具から四角いスポットライトがテーブルに注いでいる

The 1st floor dining room; square spotlights are cast onto the tables from the onyx lighting equipment.

スライド プロジェクターで貝の形を壁面に写し出す演出があちらこちらにみえる

The shell shapes are presented on the wall here and there by using a slide projector.

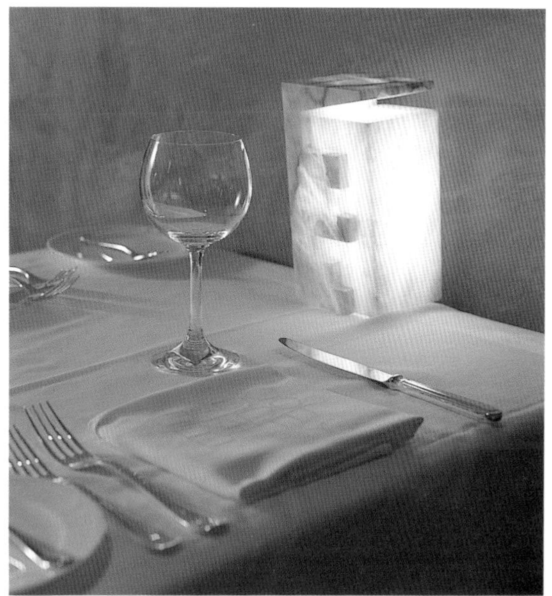

ユニークなテーブルランプ とテーブルセッティング

The unique table lamp.

エルドラド プチ

スペインのバルセロナとコスタブラバにある同レストランの海外出店の1号店。"ローマ人の影響を受けたというスペイン カタロニア地方の料理を知ってもらうのが願い"とオーナーのクルアナス(Cruañas)氏は言う。スペインの北東部に位置するカタロニア地方は 古くからイタリアやフランスとの交流も盛んで 独自の料理を生み出している所。このニューヨーク店では よりコンテンポラリーなメニューにしている。インテリアは スペインの建築家Roberto PalliとJamie Tresserraによるウルトラモダンのデザイン。160席の店内は2層に分けられ 1階はアースカラーの壁面にスライド プロジェクターによる貝のパターンの投写やオニキスの照明器具がユニーク。1階バーコーナーや 2階ダイニングエリアは 磨き上げられた自然木とモダンな家具が素晴らしい。

開店　:1990年6月8日
営業時間:午前11時30分～午後2時30分(月～金 ランチ)
午後6時～11時(月～土 ディナー)
客席数 :160席
従業員数:57名

ELDORADO PETIT

This is the first overseas branch of "Eldorado Petit" which already operates in Barcelona and Costa Brava, Spain. The owner Cruañas says that he wishes his customers to become familiar with the food in the Catalonian district of Spain, which is said to have been influenced by the Romans. Since olden times, Catalonia, which is situated in the northeastern part of Spain, has continued to be closely tied with Italy, France, etc., creating its own unique cuisine.

The New York branch however offers a more contemporary menu. The interior features an ultra modern design undertaken by the Spanish architects Roberto Palli and Jamie Tresserra. The interior has 160 seats divided into two levels, and the 1st floor features shell patterns cast by a slide projector on the earth-colored wall and onyx lighting equipment. The 1st floor corner bar and 2nd floor dining area wonderfully finished with polished natural wood and modern furniture.

Opened : June 8, 1990
Hours : 11:30 a.m. to 2:30 p.m. (lunch – Monday to Friday)
6:00 p.m. to 11:00 p.m. (dinner – Monday to Saturday)
Capacity : 160 seats
Number of employees: 57

カタロニア料理をより洗練されたコンテンポラリーな料理にし ニューヨーカーたちの心をつかもうとして出店したレストラン

The restaurant intends to capture the heart of New Yorkers by arranging Catalonian foods into more contemporary foods.

星をデザインしたフロアとスペイン調のサービス テーブル

Spanish service tables and the floor which is designed with star patterns.

2階のダイニングエリア　ウルトラモダンのスペイン家具や照明　磨き上げた自然木などで構成している
The 2nd floor dining area; composed of ultra-modern Spanish furniture and lighting equipment, polished natural wood, etc.

地中海ブルーを使用したトイレのデザイン
The toilet design using the Mediterranean blue.

トイレの入口前の壁面にも貝が写しだされている
Shell images projected on the wall in front of the entrance to the toilet.

①

②

③

④

1/ Stuffed Seafood Red Peppers with Vegetable Sauce.
2/ Salted Codfish Salad with White Beans.
3/ Black Bass Roasted with Potatoes & Rosemary.
4/ Fresh Chevre with honey and Pine Nuts.

アメリカを代表するシェフの一人・Larry Forgione氏は　国内産の素材にこだわり　新しい感覚のアメリカ料理を提供している
Larry Forgione, one of the representative American chefs, clinging to domestic ingredients, offers new-sense American foods.

An American Place

2 Park Avenue on 32nd New York, N. Y. 10016
Phone/212-684-2122

右/32ndストリートとパークアベニューの交差点近くにある赤いテントのファサード
Right / The red-tented facade near the intersection of the 32nd Street and Park Avenue.

Nancy Mah氏によるアールデコのデザイン　店内にはデキシーランド ジャズが流れ　店名の如くアメリカを強調する雰囲気がいっぱい

The art deco design made by Nancy Mah; in the restaurant Dixieland jazz is on air, and as the name suggests, "An American Place" is filled with an atmosphere which strongly stresses "America."

アットホームな店内には現代アーティストの絵画が多く飾られている
The homely interior is densely decorated with paintings by contemporary artists.

アン アメリカン プレイス

アメリカを代表するシェフの一人　ラリー フォージオーネ(Larry Forgione)氏が経営する"アメリカ"そのものを主張したレストランである。ロングアイランド生まれのフォージオーネ氏は　いままで家庭料理で食べられていたものが数多く忘れられていることを憂え　こだわりをもって国内産の食材のみを使用し　古いレシピィに彼独自のインスピレーションを加えた新しいアメリカ料理を考えだした。彼は1983年にアッパー イースト サイド(Upper East Side)にフォーマルなレストランとしてオープンしたが　パークアベニューに移り　よりカジュアルな雰囲気の店にして　予約なしのワインやアペタイザー　デザートだけの客も歓迎している。店内にはデキシーランドジャズが流れ　ナンシー マー(Nancy Mah)によるアールデコのインテリアと　アメリカ調の民芸家具や椅子　現代絵画などが見られる。バーエリアではカウンターやテーブルに伝統的なアメリカン ポテトチップスがのせられている。

開　　店：1989年2月
営業時間：午前11時45分～午後3時(ランチ　月～金)
　　　　　午後5時30分～10時(ディナー　月～土)
客 席 数：125席
従業員数：25～30名
客 単 価：ランチ/25ドル　ディナー/45～50ドル

AN AMERICAN PLACE

A restaurant asserting "America" itself, "An American Place" is managed by Larry Forgione, one of the leading American chefs. Born in Long Island, Mr. Forgione felt sorry that many family foods had been forgotten, and by particularly choosing domestic materials alone, he created new American foods by adding his own inspiration to old recipes. At first, he opened the restaurant in 1983 on the Upper East Side as a formal restaurant, but thereafter moved to Park Avenue to open a more casual restaurant, accepting even those guests who came to enjoy wine, appetizers or just desserts without reservations. In the restaurant Dixieland jazz is on the air, and one sees Nancy Mah's art deco interior, and pieces of American folk art furniture and chairs plus contemporary paintings. At the bar, traditional American potato chips are placed on the counter and tables.

Opened : February 1989
Hours : 11:45 a.m. to 3:00 p.m. (lunch – Monday to Friday)
5:30 p.m. to 10:00 p.m. (dinner – Monday to Saturday)
Capacity : 125 seats
Number of employees : 25 to 30
Price per customer : lunch/$25, dinner/$45 to $50

店内奥からバー方向をみる　椅子のデザインもユニーク

The bar corner viewed from an inner part; the chairs are also designed uniquely.

モザイク模様がカラフルなタイルフロアのバーエリア

The bar area whose floor is finished with colorful mosaic tiles.

テーブルに伝統的なアメリカン ポテトチップスを置くバー

The bar with traditional American potato chips on the tables.

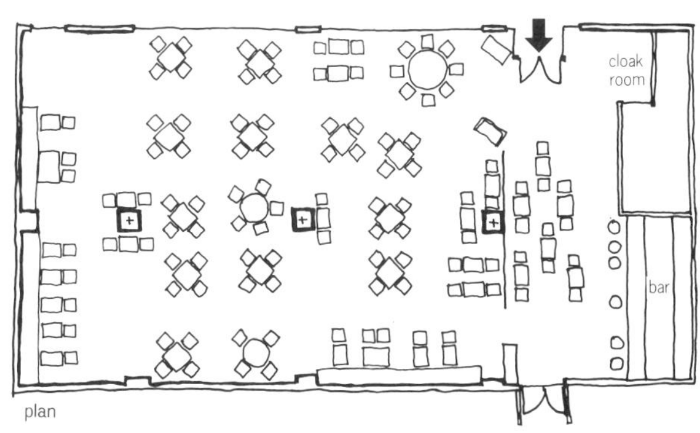

①

③

②

④

1/ BARBECUED HAWAIIAN MAHI SALAD WITH TROPICAL SALSA.
2/ WARM ROASTED VIDALLIA SALAD WITH HONY MUSTARD VINAIGRETTE.
3/ CRISP ADIRONDACK FREE RANGE DUCK GLAZED WITH WILD FLOWER HONEY with mild roast garlic whipped potatoes and natural jus.
4/ WHITE CHOCOLATE and RASPBERRY NAPOLEON with coconut crisp and candied lemon peel.

エントランス廻り　カジュアルなカフェスタイル

The entrance area; in a casual cafe style.

21 East 16th Street New York, N.Y. 10003
Phone/212-243-4020

ファサード　美しい建物が並ぶフラットアイアン地区(Flatiron District)にある

The facade; situated in Flatiron District where beautiful buildings stand in a row.

バーコーナー　ワインのコレクションが多いのでも有名

The bar corner; also famous for a wine collection which includes various types.

左/レセプション　その後方はバーコーナー

Left / The reception behind which the bar corner lies.

ダイニングルーム　カリフォルニア スタイルのビストロといったカジュアルな雰囲気で　現代アートのコレクションが多く飾られている
The dining room; looks like a bistro in Californian style, and in a casual atmosphere pieces of contemporary art are densely displayed.

ユニオン スクエア カフェ

ニューヨークの中で最も美しい建物が建ち並ぶ歴史のある環境を持つフラットアイアン地区とユニオン スクエア パークに挟まれた5番街（Fifth Avenue）周辺をソフィー（South of Fifthの略）と呼び　このレストランもその中に位置する。有名出版社　広告代理店　芸術家のスタジオ　ブティックなどが多くあり　ソフィスティケイトされた人たちが移り住んでいる地域でもある。ランチタイムには周辺の会社のビジネスマンが多く　パワーランチで連日満席である。ニューヨークのレストラン サーベイ誌"Zagat"によれば　最も好きなレストランの7位にランクされ　人気は毎年上昇している。料理はイタリアとフランスの流れを受けたアメリカ料理で　新鮮な素材が使用され豊富なワインのコレクションとあわせ好評である。カリフォルニア スタイルのビストロといったカジュアルな雰囲気の店内には　現代アートのコレクションが飾られている。またこのレストランの人気をささえているのは　従業員たちのフレンドリーな接客態度と料理やワインに対する知識の豊富さである。これはオーナーのダニー メヤー（Danny Mayer）氏を中心にしたスタッフたちのミーティングと独自の採用システムによるものである。

開　　店：1985年10月20日
営業時間：正午～午後2時30分（ランチ 月～土）
　　　　　午後6時～10時30分（ディナー 月～木 金・土は11時30分まで）
客 席 数：130席
従業員数：74名
客 単 価：ランチ/30ドル　ディナー/45ドル

UNION SQUARE CAFE

Sandwiched by the Flatiron area which features a historical environment with rows of the most beautiful buildings in New York and Union Square Park, an area around Fifth Avenue is called "Sofi" (abbreviation of South of Fifth), and the restaurant "Union Square Cafe" is situated there. It is also an area used by many well-known publishers, advertising agents, artists' studios, boutiques, etc., and many sophisticated people moved there to reside. At lunchtime, the restaurant is used by many businessmen from neighboring companies who come to have a "power lunch," and all seats are occupied everyday. According to "Zagat," a restaurant survey magazine in New York, the "Union Square Cafe" is ranked 7th on the list of most favorite restaurants in New York, and is becoming more popular every year. The menu consists of American cuisine affected by Italian and French styles, and features the use of fresh materials which are favorably accepted together with a rich collection of wine. In the restaurant which has a casual atmosphere like a bistro Californian style, a collection of pieces of contemporary art are displayed. The restaurant's popularity is also supported by the employees' friendly attitude towards guests and their rich stock of knowledge about foods and wine. This is due to the instructional meetings of the staff centering around the owner Danny Mayer and the restaurant's own recruiting system.

Opened : October 20, 1985
Hours : noon to 2:30 p.m. (lunch – Monday to Saturday)
6:00 p.m. to 10:30 p.m. (dinner – Monday to Thursday, till 11:30 p.m. on Friday and Saturday)
Capacity : 130 seats
Number of employees: 74
Price per customer : lunch/$30, dinner/$45

イタリアとフランス料理の流れを受けたアメリカ料理を提供し　連日満席の賑い
Serving American foods which are influenced by Italian and French foods, the restaurant is filled to capacity everyday.

大きな壁面アートのある1階のダイニングルーム

The 1st floor dining room featuring a large wall art.

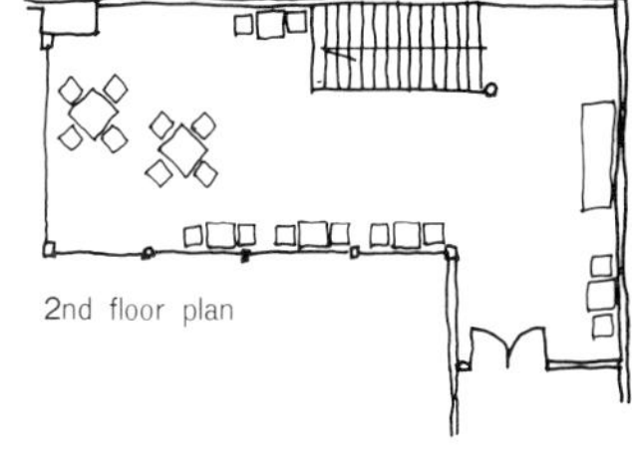

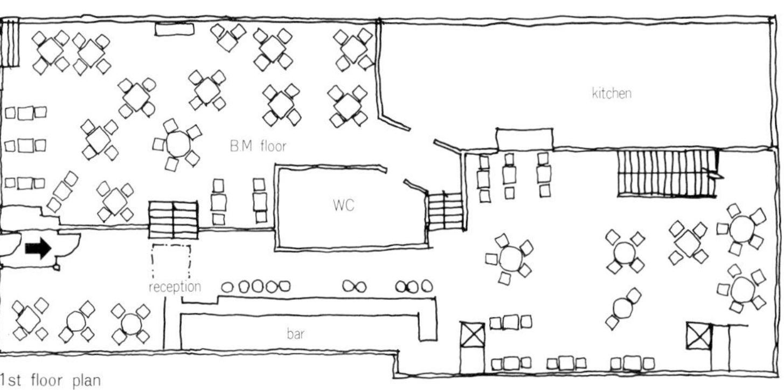

大きなイラストの下に展開するテーブル席とサービスステーション

The table seating area and service station arranged under a large illustration.

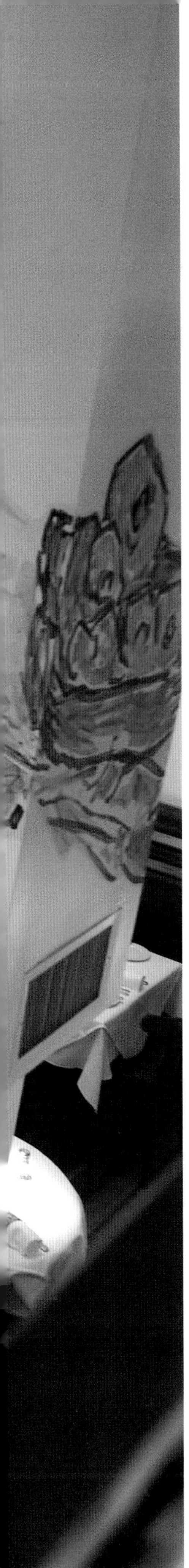

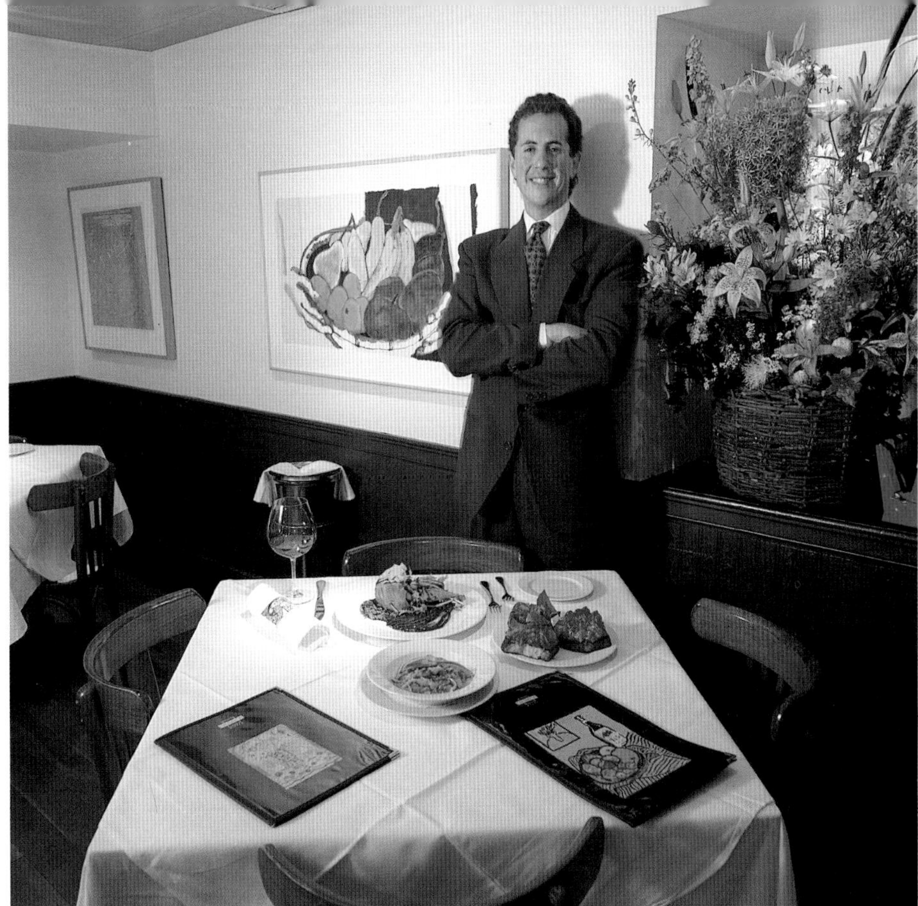

従業員教育やオペレーション　すべてに細心の努力を重ね人気を勝ち取ったオーナーの Danny Meyer 氏
The owner Danny Meyer who has won popularity by continuing careful efforts in employee education, operation and all other aspects of restaurant management.

①

③

②

1/ Bruschetta Rossa- Garlic-Rubbed Grilled Sourdough with Tomatoes, Basil and Tuscan Olive Oil.
2/ Union Square Cafe's "Pappardelle" of Green market Zuccinis with Light Tomato Sauce and Wilted Squash Blossoms.
3/ Union Square Cafe's Grilled Marinated Fillet Mignon of Tuna with Grilled Eggplant & Mustard Greens.

「Doral Park Hotel」の1階にあるレストランへのエントランスホール

The entrance hall to the restaurant on the 1st floor of "Doral Park Hotel."

Saturnia
RESTAURANT • BAR

54 Varick Street New York, N.Y. 10013
Phone/212-966-1239

白と黒で統一したバーコーナー

The bar corner uniformly finished with black & white.

入口からバーとレストランをみる

The bar and restaurant viewed from the entrance.

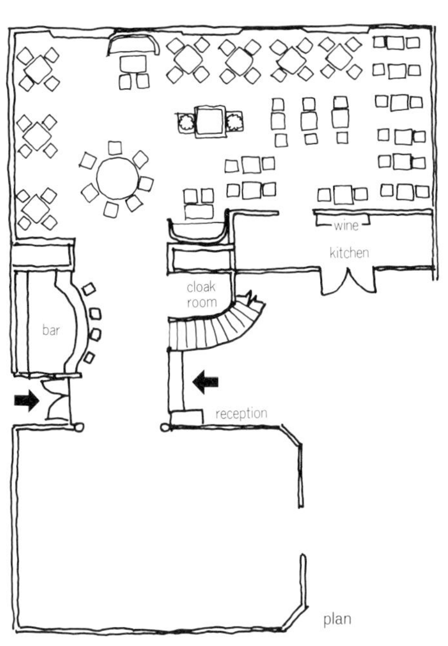

デザイナー・Sarah Lee氏による ヨーロッパ調のエレガントなデコア

European elegant decor designed by designer Sarah Lee.

サターニア

健康と食生活の関係は深く 多くの人たちの関心事である。そんなダイエット フードを提供するレストランが「サターニア」。このレストランで使用しているメニューの どの料理にもカロリー数と脂肪値（ファットポイント――F.P.）が記されており 塩分 蛋白質 糖分などの栄養素のバランスも考慮されている。オーダーは アペタイザー アントレ デザートの3つのカテゴリーから各1品選ぶコース料理を採用し カロリー 脂肪値がチェックされているのが特徴。料理には日常食べているあらゆる素材が使用され 肉類を避け野菜をといった片寄ったダイエット指向でなく 素材の分量を制限し なおバランスのあるボリュームや視覚的に満足感のある料理を開発している。

インテリアはグレコ ローマン風の庭園を壁面に描いたエレガントな造りになっている。

開店　:1990年9月20日

営業時間:午前6時30分～10時30分(朝食)

　正午～午後3時(月～金　ランチ)

　午後6時30分～10時30分(月～土　ディナー)

客席数　:70席　バー5席

客単価　:29ドル(コースメニューのみ――飲物別/朝食除く)

SATURNIA

Health and eating habits are deeply related to each other, and have remained the concern of many people. "Saturnia" is a "restaurant" which offers diet food for such people. All of the items on the menu used in the restaurant come with a caloric value and fat point (F.P.), as well as a nutrient balance with such ingredients as salt, protein and sugar indicated. A course ordering system is employed which selects one each from the three categories – appetizer, entrée and dessert – upon checking the caloric value and F. P. By using ingredients which are eaten daily, the chef intends to create dishes which are limited in the type of ingredients used, but balanced, voluminous, and pleasing to the eye – without pursuing lopsided diet food which, for instance, exclusively uses vegetables, while avoiding meat.

The interior is elegantly finished by with Greco-Roman paintings on the wall.

Opened : September 20, 1990

Hours : 6:30 a.m. to 10:30 a.m. (breakfast)

noon to 3:00 p.m. (lunch – Monday to Friday)

6:30 p.m. to 10:30 p.m. (dinner – Monday to Saturday)

Capacity : 70 seats, bar 5 seats

Price per customer : $29 (course menu alone – excluding drinks/breakfast)

栄養バランスを考えた料理を独自に開発し　健康食に対するニーズに応えるレストランとしても注目されている
"Saturnia" is also drawing attention as a restaurant which develops original dishes by taking account of nutritive balance thereby meeting the needs for health foods.

レストランからバー方向をみる
The bar area viewed from the restaurant side.

壁面にミラーを配して広がりを強調
Stresses the expanse by finishing the wall with a mirror.

グレコ ロマン(Greco-Roman)の庭園を壁面に描いたロマンチックな雰囲気のテーブル席

The table seating area having a romantic atmosphere with a Greco-Roman garden painted on the wall.

健康食でグルメ料理を開発したシェフのDerrick Dikkers氏

The chef Derrick Dikkers who developed health-oriented gourmet foods.

①

②

1/ Rolled Vegetarian Lavosh Swirl with Guacamole & Alfalfa Sprouts.
2/ Slow-Cooked Breast of Chicken with Provencale Vegetables & Turned Potatoes.

Canal Streetのすぐ南側にあり　トライベッカ地区のベジタリアンたちに話題のレストラン

Just south of Canal Street, "NOSMO KING" is a restaurant hotly talked about by vegetarians in the Tribeca area.

NOSMO KING

70 West 68th Street New York, N. Y. 10023
Phone/212-721-0068

ロゴ入りのTシャツも売っている

Logo-marked T-shirts are also on sale.

2階のプライベート ダイニングからレストラン全景をみる 店頭の大きな窓はブラインドによって光を調整できる

The entire appearance of the restaurant viewed from the private dining room on the 2nd floor; the large shop-front window can adjust incoming light with a blind.

ダークウッドのパネルとコーディネートされたテーブル席　壁面にはアンティークの絵画や置物が飾られている
The table seating area coordinated with dark wood panels; the wall is decorated with antique paintings and ornaments.

バーに隣接したブース席　The booth seating area adjacent to the bar.

レセプション際からバーエリアをみる

The bar area viewed from the reception area.

ノズモ キング

店名のユニークさ 店内いっぱいに飾られたアンティークのアートや置き物 各種のカップで構成されたウッドパネルのダイニングルーム そして有機栽培による自家製野菜を使用した料理などが主な特徴。キャナル ストリート(Canal Street)のすぐ南に位置するトライベッカ(Tribeca)地区の話題のレストランで 多くのベジタリアンが足を運ぶ。料理はシェフのアラン ハーディング(Alan Harding)氏がつくる芸術的な盛りつけの心のこもったコンテンポラリースタイルの料理で 開店以来 口伝えに広まったものという。ディナーのみの営業だが ケイタリング サービスもしている。店内に飾られている絵画や置き物は ほとんどが オーナーのスティーブ フランケル(Steve Frankel)氏の収集したもので 希望すれば購入可能である。落ち着いた居心地の良いレストランである。

開　　店:1989年8月16日
営業時間:午後6時～11時(ディナー)
客 席 数:60席
従業員数:15名
客 単 価:35ドル(飲物及びサービス料を含む)

NOSMO KING

Having a unique name, the restaurant also features antique pieces of art and ornaments displayed all over the interior, a dining room finished with wood panels and equipped with various cups, and also dishes using homemade vegetables cultured by using organic fertilizers. Frequently talked about in the Tribeca area which is just south of Canal Street, "Nosmo King" is frequented by many vegetarians. The contemporary styled cuisine is dished out heartily by the chef Alan Harding and news of the restaurant has been handed down by word of mouth since the opening. Although service is limited to dinnertime, catering is available. Almost all paintings and ornaments have been collected by the owner Steve Frankel, and can be purchased upon request. The restaurant is composed and comfortable.

Opened : August 16, 1989
Hours : 6:00 p.m. to 11:00 p.m. (dinner)
Capacity : 60 seats
Number of employees: 15
Price per customer : $35 (including drinks and service charge)

有機栽培による自家製野菜を使用し　芸術的な盛り付　心のこもったコンテンポラリー スタイルの料理を提供している　店頭に置かれたワゴン車はケイタリング用

By using homemade vegetables cultured with organic fertilizers, the restaurant offers foods dished up artistically and heartily in a contemporary style; wagons stopping in front of the restaurant are used for catering.

plan

右/シェフの Alan Harding 氏とメートルディの Traci Dutton さん

Right / The chef Alan Harding and maître d'Traci Dutton.

天窓のあるダイニング エリアをみる　ニューイングランド地方の家庭料理がメニューの中心　中央の黒板に日替りのメニューを書きこむ

The menu mainly consists of family foods in New England. A view of the dining area having a skylight; the menu, whose contents change day by day, is written on the central blackboard.

Vince & Eddies

70 Park Avenue at 38th Street New York, N. Y. 10016
Phone/212-983-3333

右/住宅街にあるレストランのファサード

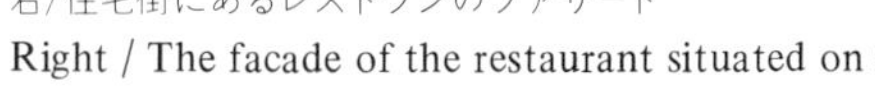

Right / The facade of the restaurant situated on a residential quarter.

家庭的な雰囲気のダイニングルーム　壁面にアンティークの絵画や写真が飾られている
The dining room in a homely atmosphere; decorated with antique paintings and photos on the wall.

ヴィンス＆エディーズ
二人の経営者の名前を店名にした「ヴィンス＆エディーズ」は　ニューイングランド地方の家庭料理を提供し　ニューヨークのアッパーウエストサイド(Upper West Side)のリンカーンセンター近くに位置する。ヤッピーたちが多く住む地域であり　周囲には彼等を対象としたトレンディな人気のあるレストランやブティックが多くある。'80年代後半よりアメリカの家庭料理　いわゆる"おふくろの味"がクローズアップされ　シンプルでボリュームのある料理に人気がでてきている。メニューは説明書きがなくても理解でき　安心して注文できるものばかりで　ホームクッキングから　さらにグレードアップされた料理で評判である。デザインはサム ロパタ(Sam Lopata)で　暖炉や大家族用のテーブル　アンティークの柱時計や写真　絵画などがとりいれられ　家庭的な雰囲気になっている。これは郊外でよく見かけるイン(旅篭)を思い起こさせる造りだ。これらのアンティークの調度品や絵画などは希望すれば購入することもできる。

開店　　:1990年10月10日
営業時間:正午～午後3時(ランチ)
　　　　　午後5時30分～午後11時(ディナー)
客席数　:65席
従業員数:31名
客単価　:ランチ/16ドル50セント　ディナー/32ドル50セント

VINCE & EDDIE'S

Situated near Lincoln Center of the Upper West Side in New York city, "Vince & Eddie's," which uses the names of two managers, features New England family food. Many Yuppies live in the area and there are many popular and trendy restaurants and boutiques catering to them. Since the latter half of the '80s, American home food – so-called "mom's cooking" – have been in the limelight with simple and voluminous dishes gaining in popularity. The menu can be understood without explanation, and all items can be easily ordered ranging from home-cooked to upgraded dishes.
Designed by Sam Lopata, the interior employs a fireplace, tables for big families, antique clocks, photos, paintings, etc. so that a homelike atmosphere is produced. The interior reminds one of an inn which is often seen in the suburbs. These antique utensils, paintings, etc. can also be purchased if one desires.

Opened : October 10, 1990
Hours : noon to 3:00 p.m. (lunch)
5:30 p.m. to 11:00 p.m. (dinner)
Capacity : 65 seats
Number of employees: 31
Price per customer : lunch/$15.50, dinner/$32.50

サマータイムにはガラスの扉の外にある中庭を開放し　テーブル席が増席される

During summer time, the courtyard outside the glass door is opened and capacity of the table seating area is increased.

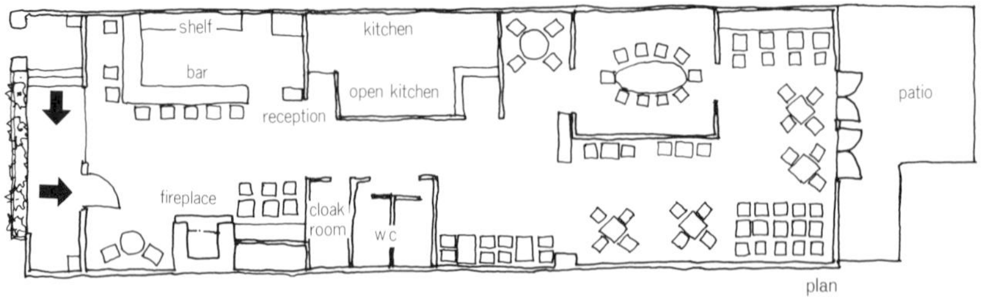

左/エントランス際のバーは落ち着いたホームバー的な雰囲気

Left / The bar beside the entrance has a composed atmosphere like that of a home bar.

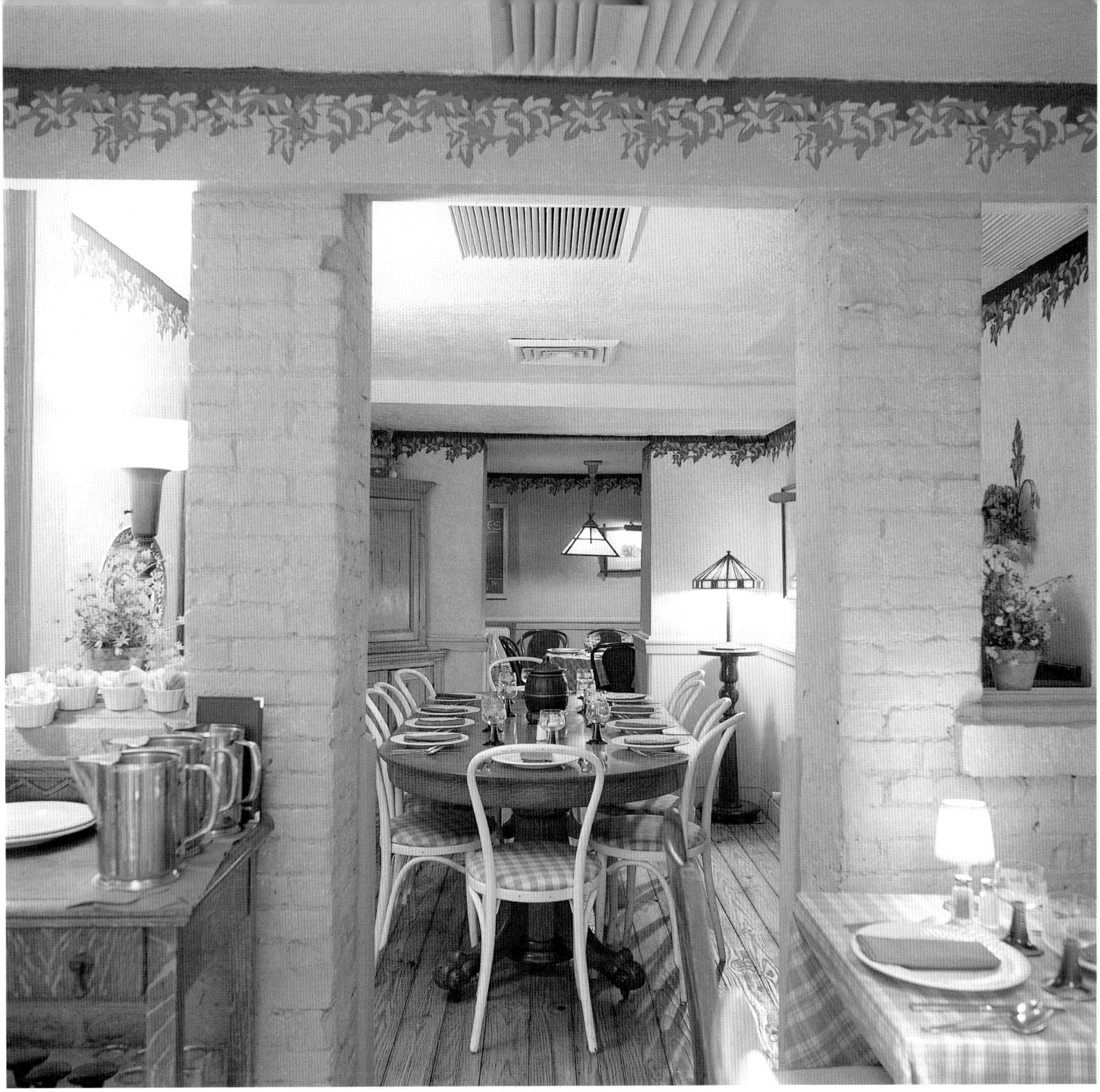

大家族用のテーブルがある部屋　壁面は黄色　椅子は白と他の部屋の雰囲気と変えている

A room having a table for large family use; using yellow on the wall and white on the chairs, the room is differentiated in atmosphere from the other rooms.

暖炉のあるバーコーナー

The bar corner equipped with a fireplace.

キッチンの際にあるダイニングエリア

The dining area beside the kitchen.

グレードアップしたアメリカの家庭料理を手掛けるシェフのScott Cambell氏(左)
パートナーのSteven Tollen氏(中) シェフのDavid Ramer氏

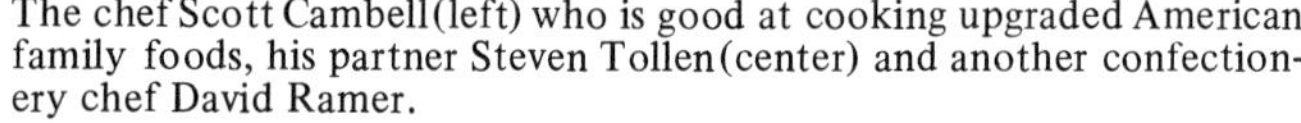

The chef Scott Cambell(left) who is good at cooking upgraded American family foods, his partner Steven Tollen(center) and another confectionery chef David Ramer.

②

①

③

1/ Gravlax Salad with Mini Lettuces & Mustard Mayo.
2/ Salad Nicoise & with Mini Greens, Black Olive Sauce, Grilled Canadian Salmon.
3/ Pan Roasted Chicken with Savoy Cabbage & Roasted Garlic Sauce.

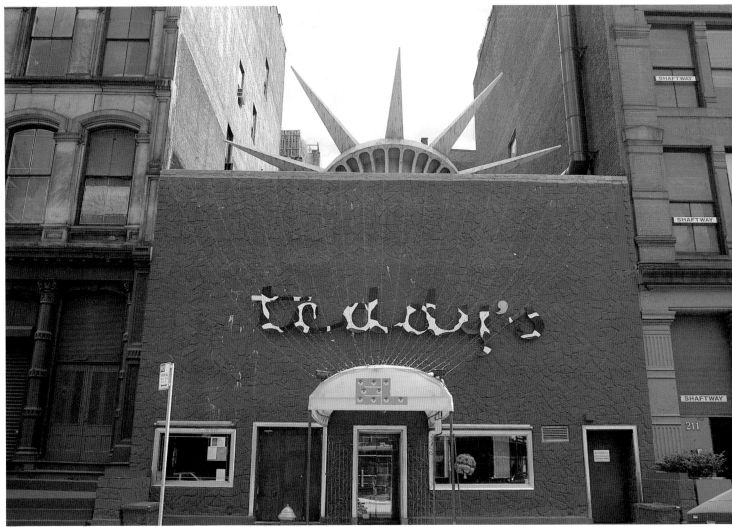

1980年代　タパス料理で話題となったあの「El Internacional」の面影を残すファサード

The facade still retains some vestige of “El Internacional” which was hotly talked about in the mid-1980s.

各種木材の切れ端で作ったミラーのフレームがあるホールウェイ

The mirror-framed hallway made by using chips of various types of wood.

N.Y.のトレンディなマガジンを置くラックがダイニングに通じる通路にある

By the aisle leading to the dining room there is a rack to display trendy magazines in New York.

teddy's

219 West Broadway New York, N.Y. 10013
Phone/212-941-7070

鉄製コイルや古いレジスターで作った階段の手摺り　壁面に沿った2本のＢＢＱの串など　新旧のアートワークが交差するイノベーティブな店内

The staircase's handrails made by using steel coils, old resistors, etc. Coupled with two barbecue skewers, etc., the interior forms an innovative space where new and old artworks mingle with each other.

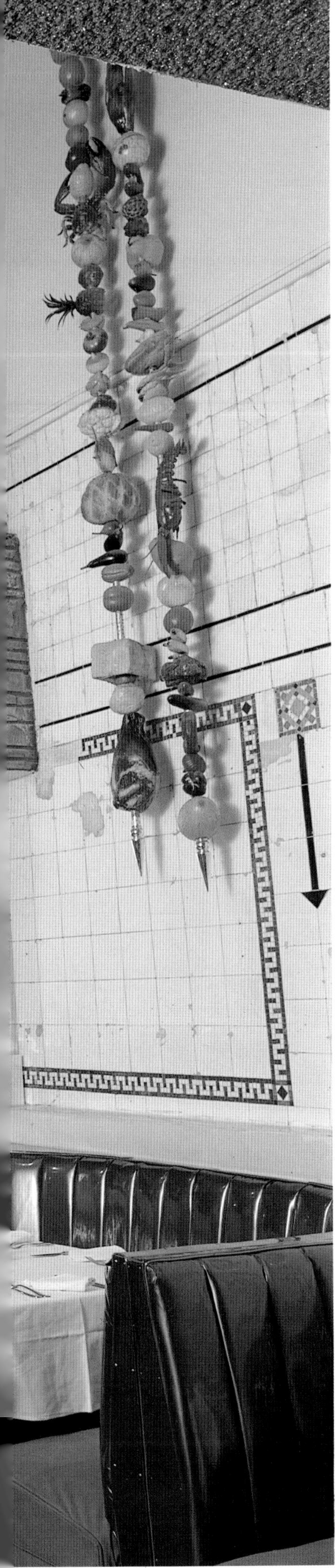

現代アートの手摺りを通してダイニングルームをみる
The dining room viewed across the handrails which come as a piece of modern art.

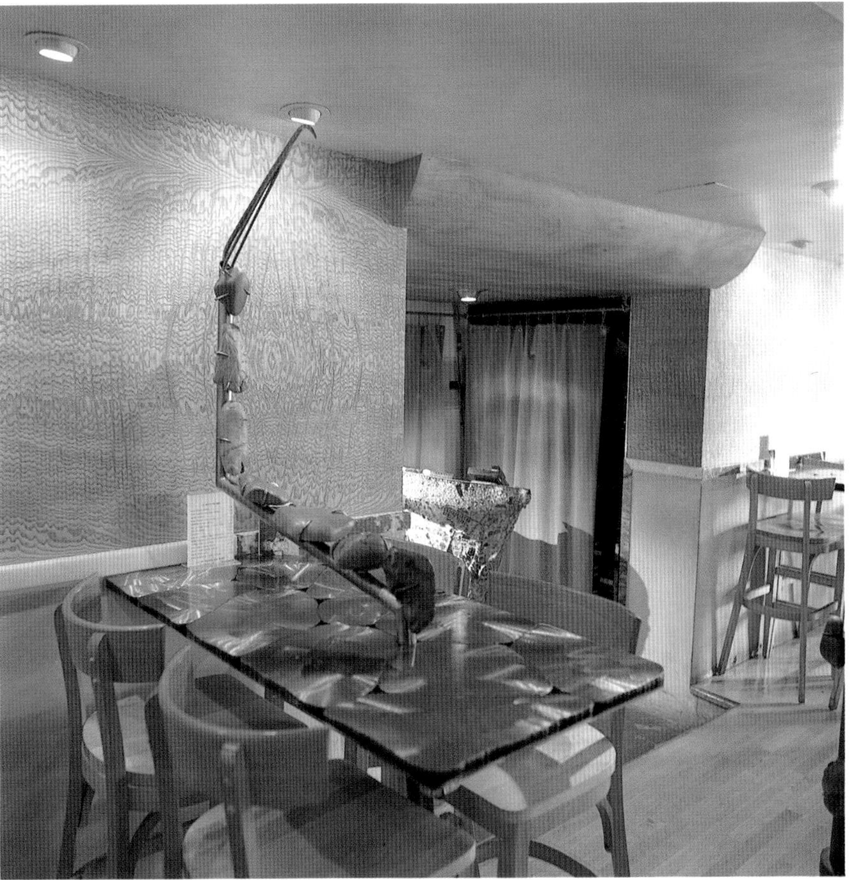

バーエリアのテーブルにスティールと丸石で構成する作品がある
On the table at the bar area there is a piece of artwork which is composed of steel and cobbles.

1940年代の壁紙で構成するダイニングルーム

The dining room whose interior is composed of the 1940s wall papers.

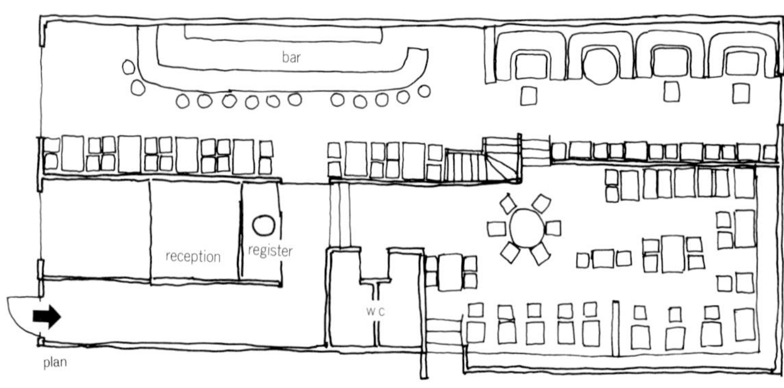

右/アップスケールなメキシコ料理を提供するレストラン

Right / The restaurant serving upscale Mexican foods.

ダイニングルームのユニークなアート作品

Unique pieces of artwork in the dining room.

エル テディーズ

ニューヨークの本格的なメキシカン レストランを目指し アンドリュウ ヤング(Andrew Young)氏とクリストファー チェスナット(Cristopher Chesnutt)氏が トライベッカ地区(Tribeca)にオープンしたのが「エル テディーズ」。元々この建物は テディーという人によって 1925年に始められたカフェテリアからステーキハウス タパス料理など種々のレストランに経営が変わっていったという長い歴史のあるもの。自由の女神の巨大なクラウン(冠)を 屋根の上に乗せたユニークなファサードは 1980年代半ばにオープンし話題になったタパス料理のレストラン「エル インターナショナル(El Internacional)」の それを引き継いだものである。店内にもカフェテリア当時のタイルの壁画やモザイクの壁が そのまま残されている。古き良き歴史のあるものとアーティストたちによる モダンアート感覚の作品によって新しいインテリアに生まれ変わっている。料理は伝統的なメキシコ料理を中心に その日の入荷によって変わる日替わりやベジタリアン向けメニューなど 新鮮な食材を使用した独自のメニューを開発している。

開店　　:1989年1月12日

営業時間:正午～午後2時30分(月～金 ランチ)
午後6時～11時30分(月～木 ディナー)
午後6時～午前1時(金・土 ディナー)

客席数　:100席

従業員数:30名

客単価　:24ドル

バーからダイニングルームをみる 正面にオープンキッチンがみえる

The dining room viewed from the bar; one sees the open kitchen right in front of oneself.

EL TEDDY'S

Specifically operated as an orthodox Mexican restaurant in New York, "El teddy's" was opened in Tribeca by Andrew Young and Cristopher Chesnutt. The building itself has a long history, as there was a cafeteria inside which was started in 1925 by an operator named Teddy. It then changed to a steak house, tapas restaurant, etc. The unique facade has a huge crown of the Statue of Liberty and was taken over from the tapas restaurant "El Internacional" which opened in the mid-1980s. The interior retains the tiled frescos and mosaic walls which had been installed in the cafeteria days. The interior which is reminiscent of the "good old days" is combined with a modern artistic sense produced by contemporary artists, thus bringing about an attractive interior finish. The menu mainly consists of traditional Mexican food, and vegetarian food which changes from day to day according to the materials available on the day. Thus, the restaurant's own unique menu has been developed by using fresh ingredients.

Opened : January 12, 1989
Hours : noon to 2:30 p.m.
(lunch – Monday to Friday)
6:00 p.m. to 11:30 p.m.
(dinner – Monday to Thursday)
6:00 p.m. to 1:00 a.m.
(dinner – Friday and Saturday)
Capacity : 100 seats
Number of employees : 30
Price per customer : $24

①

②

③

④

1/ Arugula, Roasted Red Pepper & Jicama Salad.
2/ Grilled Salmon with Roasted Red Pepper Salsa.
3/ Grilled Turkey Breast with Mole Poblano and Chilaquile.
4/ Shrimps with Garlic Cream.

エントランスから店内をみる　右がバー　中央がダイニングルーム　奥にオープンキッチン

The interior viewed from the entrance; the bar (right), the dining room (center), and the open kitchen (behind).

Broadway Grill

49th Street & Broadway, Holiday Inn Crowne Plaza 2F, New York, N. Y.
Phone/212-315-6161

「Holiday Inn Crowne Plaza」の2階にある開放的なファサード

The open-type facade which has appeared on the 2nd floor of "Holiday Inn Crowne Plaza."

スポットライトに照らされたバーエリア　ミネラルウォーターなどを揃えたアクアバーとして売り出す計画もある
The spotlighted bar area; there is a plan to sell it as an aqua bar provided with mineral water, etc.

ブロードウェイ グリル

クッキー王と呼ばれる「David's Cookies」の創始者　デービッド リーダーマン(David Liederman)氏がオープンしたカジュアルなグリルレストラン。ホリディ イン クラウン プラザ ホテルの2階で　周辺にはミュージカル劇場やオフィスビルが建ち並ぶ場所に位置している。店内は中央に舞台を思わせるような　大型のオープンキッチンを配し　ロースターやグリルを全面に見せている。高級レストランが低迷ぎみのアメリカの外食事情の中で　調理法をグリルやローストといった方法に変え　安価でシンプルな料理を提供し人気を呼んでいる。

開店　店:1991年4月28日
営業時間:正午～午後5時(ランチ)
　　　　午後5時30分～午前0時(ディナー)
客 席 数:192席
従業員数:40名

BROADWAY GRILL

A casual grill type restaurant opened by David Liederman, founder of "David's Cookies," who is called the Cookie King, the "Broadway Grill" is situated on the 2nd floor of the newly built Holiday Inn Crowne Plaza Hotel on Times Square, which is surrounded with musical theaters, office buildings, etc. In the center of the interior a large open kitchen, which just looks like a stage, is installed, allowing guests to enjoy viewing the roaster, grill, etc. In the American dining-out business in which upscale restaurants remain somewhat dull, the "Broadway Grill" is gaining popularity for its cheap and simple foods cooked on a grill or by roasting.

Opened : April 28, 1991
Hours : noon to 5:00 p.m. (lunch)
5:30 p.m. to 0:00 a.m. (dinner)
Capacity : 192 seats
Number of employees: 40

大きなオープンキッチンを客席の中央に設け　安価なグリルやロースト料理を提供している
By installing a large open kitchen in the center of the guest seating space, cheap grill or roast is served.

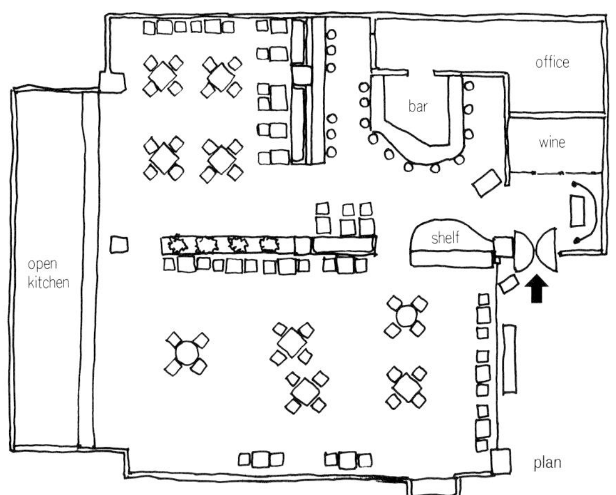

192席のカジュアルなレストラン
The casual restaurant with 192 seats.

オーナーのDavid Liederman氏はデイビッド クッキーの創始者としても有名　平均18ドルのワインを数多く揃えている
The owner David Liederman is also well known as the founder of "David's Cookies"; various types of wine – $18 on the average – are available.

①

③

②

1/ Roast Chicken "CHEZ LOUIS," with roasted garlic and fresh rosemary served with David's Potato Pie.
2/ White Bean Salad, with grilled leeks.
3/ Thin Crust Pizza
Grilled Eggplant, Zucchini, Tomato, and Fresh Mozzarella.

入口際にあるキャッシャーから店内をみる　1940～50年代をおもわせるインテリア
Looking into "EJ'S" from the cashier's desk by the entrance; the interior reminds us of the 1940s to 1960s.

433 Amsterdam Avenue New York, N. Y. 10024
Phone/212-873-3444

右/住宅街に出店し　地域に密着したレストランとして親しまれ　テイクアウトやフリー デリバリーのサービスもしている

Right / Located in a residential quarter and rooted in the community, the restaurant is loved by inhabitants, and also provides takeout or free delivery services.

テーマカラーであるブルーの椅子を配したカジュアルなテーブル席

The casual table seating area with blue (theme color) chairs.

懐かしいポスターや写真を飾る壁面
The wall used to display dear old posters and photos.

イージェイズ

アッパー ウエスト サイド(Upper West Side—80と81丁目の間)にあるキュートな感じのダイナー レストラン。周辺には小さなレストランや商店 アパートメントの住宅が多く 学生やアーティスト アクター プロフェッショナルと呼ばれる専門職などが多く住むところで これらの人たちを客層とした地域密着の気軽な雰囲気のレストラン 繁盛している。料理は おふくろの味 家庭料理などといったもので パンケーキやサンドイッチはアメリカ人なら小さい頃から食べ慣れたものであり この店の大きな皿に盛られたボリュームたっぷりの料理も人気である。ウィークデイの朝 8時前からテーブルセッティングや清掃など 準備に追われる店内を見ながら開店を待つ人たちが見られる。週末には平均400名の客が利用し ほかにテイクアウトやフリーデリバリーのサービスもある。

開　　店：1990年10月4日
営業時間：午前8時〜午後11時(月〜木 金は午前0時まで)
午前9時〜午前0時(土 日は午後11時まで)
客 席 数：60席 カウンター 8席
従業員数：30名
客 単 位：朝食/5ドル ランチ/8ドル ディナー/10ドル

学生やアーティスト アクター プロフェッショナルなどが多く利用する
Frequented by students, artists, actors, professionals, etc.

EJ'S

A diner type restaurant having a cute atmosphere, "Ej's" is situated on the Upper West Side (between 80th and 81st); it is surrounded with many small restaurants, stores and apartment houses, and the area is known for the students, artists and professionals such as "professional actors" who live there. Mainly intended for these inhabitants, "Ej's" flourishes as a community-oriented casual restaurant. The menu includes family foods associated with the taste of mom's cooking, such as pancakes and sandwiches, and voluminous foods dished out on a large plate which are very popular. On weekday mornings, one finds people even before 8:00 a.m. waiting for the opening while watching the inside where employees are busy with preparations such as table setting and cleaning. On the weekend "Ej's" is visited by 400 guests on the average. Takeout and free delivery services are also available.

Opened : October 4, 1990
Hours : 8:00 a.m. to 11:00 p.m. (Monday to Thursday, till 0:00 a.m. on Friday)
9:00 a.m. to 0:00 a.m. (Saturday, till 11:00 p.m. on Sunday)
Capacity : 60 seats, counter 8 seats
Number of employees : 30
Price per customer : breakfast/$5, lunch/$8, dinner/$10

ダイナースタイルのオープンキッチンとカウンター席をみる　このコーナーのみが喫煙席となっている

The diner-style open kitchen and counter seating area; in this corner alone, guests can smoke.

Tuna Melt Sandwich with Cole Slaw & Pickle.
EJ's Chef Salad.
Three Jumbo Butter Milk Flapjacks with Strawberries, Bananas and Blueberries.

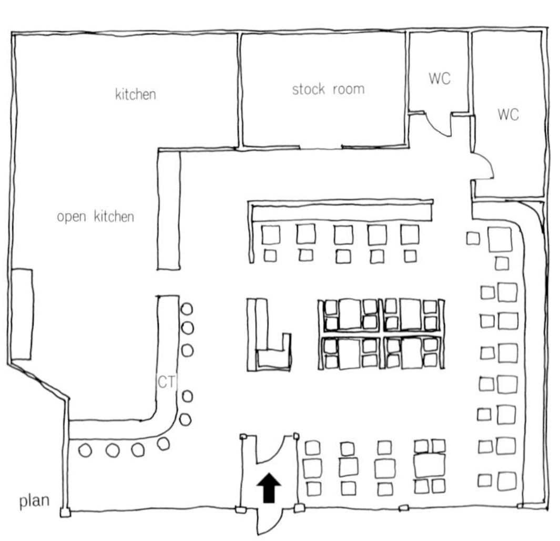

1939年に建てられたホテルのダイニングルームを　その面影を残しながらカジュアルな雰囲気のレストラン(240席)に改装したもの

The dining room of a hotel built in 1939 has been redecorated into a casual restaurant (with 240 seats) while retaining a vestige of the old dining room.

2450 Broadway New York, N. Y. 10024
Phone/212-362-2200

右/ファサード　アッパー ウエストサイドで話題となっている

Right / The facade; hotly talked about on the Upper West Side.

タイム　ライフをはじめ古い写真や絵のコレクションで演出している

Makes presentation with a collection of old covers of "Time" and "Life," photos and paintings.

カーマインズ

「カーマインズ」は　アッパー ウエスト サイド(Upper West Side)にあり料理は南イタリアとアメリカンスタイル。大皿に盛られたジャンボサイズのプレート(10～38ドル)をサービスするファミリースタイルの新しいコンセプトが人気を呼んでいる。元は1939年に建てられたホテルの広大なダイニングルームだった場所で　中国料理レストランとして27年間営業していたものを一部に面影を残して改装した。インテリアとして　タイムやライフの表紙や古い絵画　写真をフレームにして壁面に飾っている。また大きなパネルのメニューボードを掲げ　個々のテーブル席のメニューはない。無駄を省きシンプルなサービスに徹し　新鮮な魚介類を安価でたっぷりのボリュームで提供している。ディナーのみの営業で　6人以上のグループ以外の予約を受けないため　店頭近くのバーコーナーはウェイティング客でいつも混みあっている。

開　　店:1990年8月17日
営業時間:午後5時30分～11時
客 席 数:240席
客 単 価:20～25ドル

CARMINE'S

"Carmine's" is on the Upper West Side, and offers South Italian and American style foods. Their new family style concept serving a jumbo plate for $10 to $38 is gaining popularity. Originally, it was the spacious dining room of a hotel built in 1939, and after 27 years of operation as a Chinese restaurant, it was redecorated while retaining some vestige of the former restaurant. The interior features framed covers of "Time" and "Life," old paintings and photos displayed on the wall. Instead of placing a menu on each table, a large menu board (panel) is put up. Stressing simple service, "Carmine's" eliminates waste and offers a large volume of fresh fish at cheap prices. Service is limited to dinnertime and they reject reservations other than those for groups of more than 6 persons. So, the bar near the entrance is always crowded with waiting guests.

Opened : August 17, 1990
Hours : 5:30 p.m. to 11:00 p.m.
Capacity : 240 seats
Price per customer : $20 to $25

エントランス際に設けたバーコーナー　テーブルが空くまで1時間以上も待つことがある
The bar corner installed beside the entrance; sometimes guests must wait for more than an hour for vacant seats.

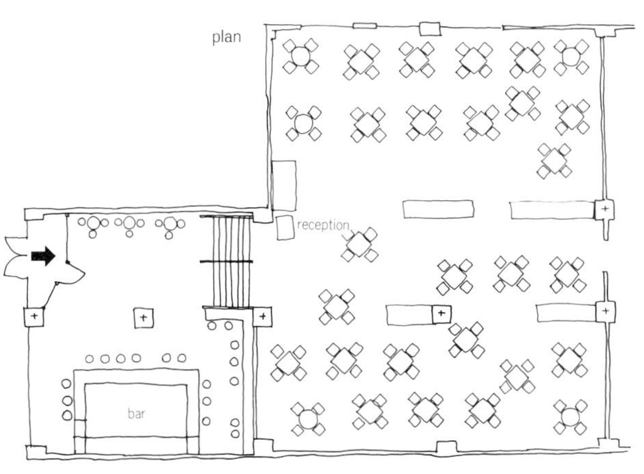

右/バー　ボトルとグラスが棚に整然と並んでいる
Right / The bar; with bottles and glass cups neatly displayed on the shelves.

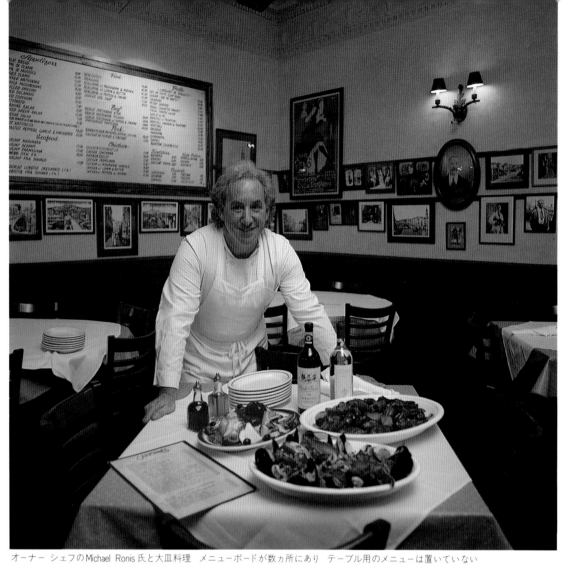

オーナー シェフのMichael Ronis氏と大皿料理 メニューボードが数ヵ所にあり テーブル用のメニューは置いていない

The owner-chef Michael Ronis and his large plate cuisine; instead of each table menu, menu boards are installed on several spots.

①

②

③

1/ Carmine Salad.
2/ Chicken Contadina.
3/ Fresh Fish of The Day.

ヨーロッパ スタイルのエレガントなエントランス ホールからロビー方向をみる

The lobby area viewed from the European styled elegant entrance hall.

NEW YORK Marriott. FINANCIAL CENTER

85 West Street New York, N.Y. 10006
Phone/212-385-4900

右/ウォール街 世界貿易センタービルなどを背景に建つ38階建て 504室のホテル

Right / 38-storied hotel with 504 rooms standing against the Wall Street, the World Trade Center, etc.

2階の宴会　会議室につづく豪華な雰囲気の階段廻り　下方にゲスト サービス デスクがみえる
The 2nd floor banquet and conference rooms, followed by the staircase area having a gorgeous atmosphere; below a guest service desk is visible.

2階のエレベーターホール　邸宅の雰囲気をだし　家具　調度品にも格調のあるものが置かれている
The 2nd floor elevator hall; having a mansion-like atmosphere, the interior is equipped with pieces of dignified furniture and fixtures.

マリオット フィナンシャル センター

アメリカを中心に全世界に約220の広いネットワークを展開するマリオット ホテルズのニューヨークにおける最新の施設である。ローアー マンハッタン(Lower Manhattan)のフィナンシャル地区に9年ぶりに登場した新しいホテルとして注目されている。ヨーロッパ スタイルのエレガントなインテリアとマリオット ホスピタリティが売りものだ。場所柄 ウォール ストリート(Wall Street) や世界貿易センター(The World Trade Center) ワールド フィナンシャル センター(World Financial Center) などのビジネス トラベラーたちをターゲットにし 宴会や会議宿泊の利用が多い。ウィークエンドには一般の観光客たちのために スペシャルウィークエンド パッケージなどのプログラムもあって 朝食付き割引価格で利用できる。上階のコンシアージ レベルにはラウンジとビジネスセンターがあり ハドソン川(Hudson River)や自由の女神像(The Statue of Liberty)が見える。

各部屋にはヘアードライヤーとデータポート(Dataport)と呼ぶコンピューターとファックス用の装置も備えられている。さらにインドア スイミングプールやサウナ エクササイズ用の器具などを備え ビジネスマンたちの健康管理の利便にも一役買っている。

開　　　業：1990年12月27日
経　　　営：Marriott Hotels, Resorts and Suites
規模・客室数：地上38階建　504室
料 飲 施 設：Jw's Restaurant/Liberty Lounge Bar & Grill
宴会・会議室：大宴会場(2)4,500 & 2,200Sq, feet/会議室(6)/ホスピタリティルーム(6)
その他施設：インドア スイミングプール/サウナ/エクササイズルーム/ギフトショップ/テレシステム(Dataport)/ビジネスセンター

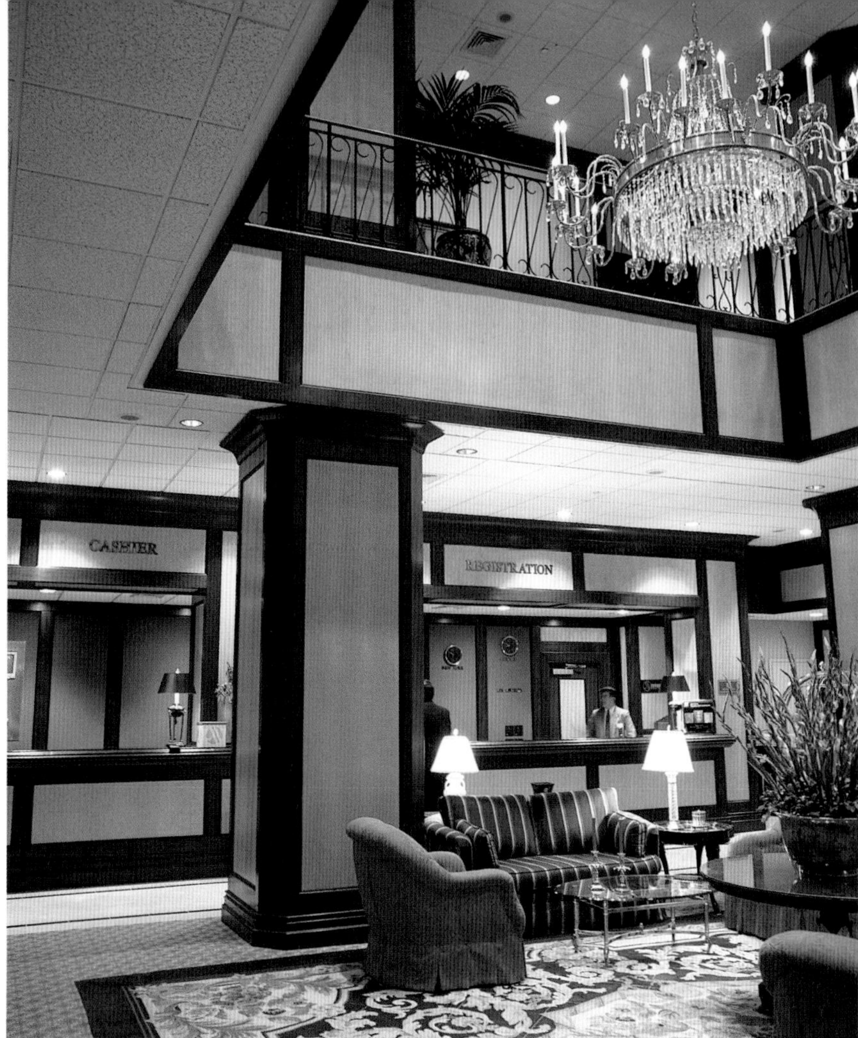

シャンデリアのある高い空間のロビーとフロント セレプション
The lobby space with chandeliers under the high ceiling, and the front reception.

MARRIOTT FINANCIAL CENTER

The latest facility in New York of the Marriott Hotel chain which is developing their network of about 220 hotels throughout the world, centering around America, the "Marriott Financial Center" is drawing attention as a new hotel that has appeared in the Financial quarter of Lower Manhattan after 9 years. It specifically features an elegant interior in the European style and Marriott's own hospitality. In view of the nature of the place, the hotel is intended to capture business travellers coming to Wall Street, the World Trade Center, World Financial Center, etc., and is heavily used by those who stay for banqueting or attending conferences. On the weekend, a special weekend package program is available for ordinary tourists who can utilize it at a discount price with breakfast. On the upper concierge level there is a lounge and business center from which the Hudson River and the Statue of Liberty are visible.

Each room is equipped with a hair drier and a device called "Dataport" for computer anf fax use, as well as kits for an indoor swimming pool, sauna, and exercise room, thus helping businessmen to better manage their health.

Opened : December 27, 1990
Management : Marriott Hotels, Resorts and Suites
Scale · number of rooms: 504 rooms
Eating & drinking facilities: Jw's Restaurant/Liberty Lounge Bar & Grill
Banquet & conference facilities: Large banquet hall (2) – 4,500 & 2,200 Sq. feet/conference room (6)/hospitality room (6)
Other facilities: Indoor swimming pool/sauna/exercise room/gift shop/tele system (Dataport)/business center

温かな色調を配したキャッシャーとレセプション
The cashier's desk and reception which are colored mildly.

1階のロビー際にある「Liberty Lounge Bar & Grill」

“Liberty Lounge Bark Grill” beside the 1st floor lobby.

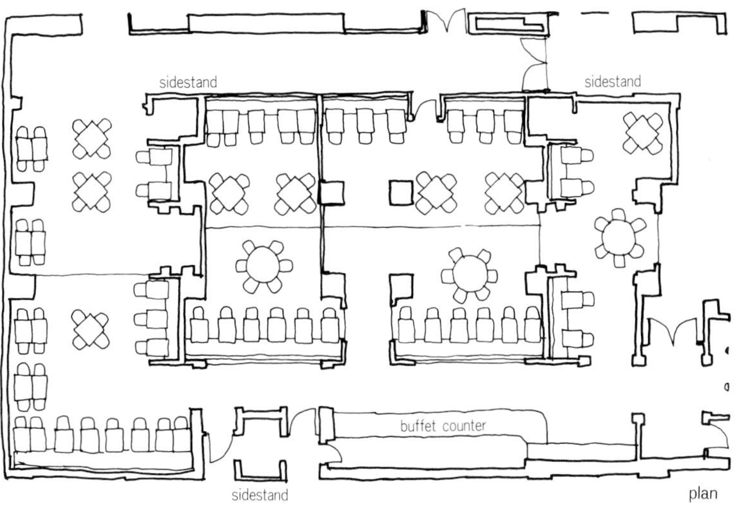

ホテル唯一のカジュアルレストラン“Jw's”は朝　昼　夜の食事を提供する

The hotel's only casual restaurant “JW'S” serves breakfast, lunch and dinner.

「Jw's」のエントランス廻り

The entrance area of “JW'S.”

このビュッフェ コーナーは近くのビジネスマンも利用している

The buffet corner is also used by nearby businessmen.

2階のFinancial Center Ballroom(2,200Sq.Ft)

"Financial Center Ballroom" (2,200 sq. ft.) on the 2nd floor.

3階の大宴会場 Grand Ballroom(4,500Sq.Ft)

The large banquet room "Grand Ballroom" (4,500 sq. ft.) on the 3rd floor.

ホテルの最上階(38F)にあるPresidential Suit room ウェットバーと小さなキッチンが付いている
"Presidential Suite Room" on the highest floor (38F) of the hotel; equipped with a wet bar and small kitchen.

リビング ルームのダイニング テーブルがあるコーナー
The living room; a corner with a dining table.

"Dataport"というテレシステムを備えるライテングデスク
The writing desk equipped with a tele-system called "Dataport."

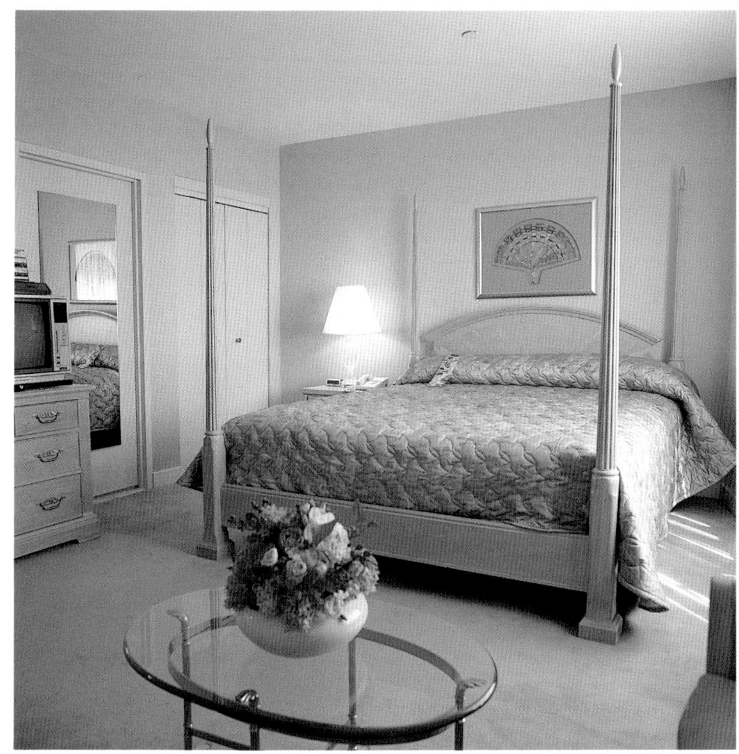

シルキーな布貼りの壁面のマスターズ ベッドルーム
"Master's Bedroom" whose wall is covered with silky cloth.

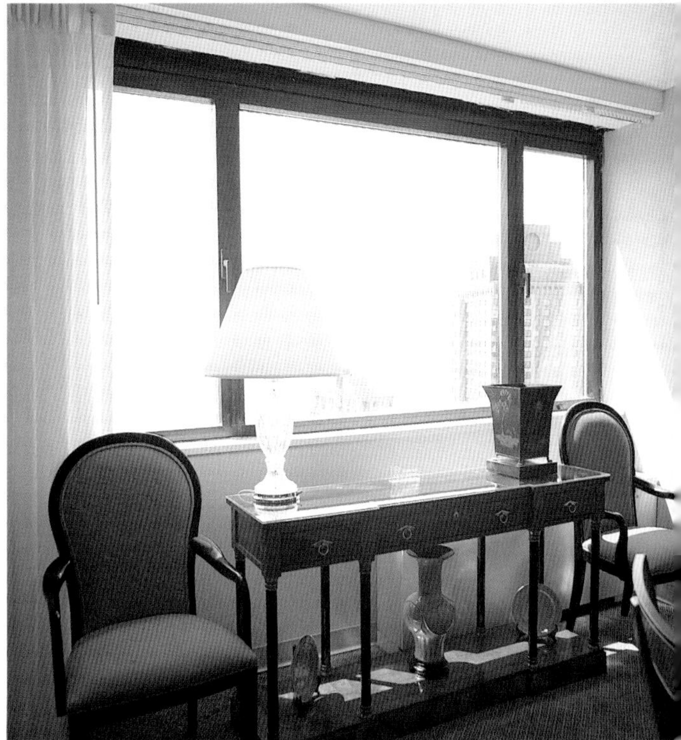

"自由の女神像"がこの窓から一望できる
From the window one can command a view of the "Statue of Liberty."

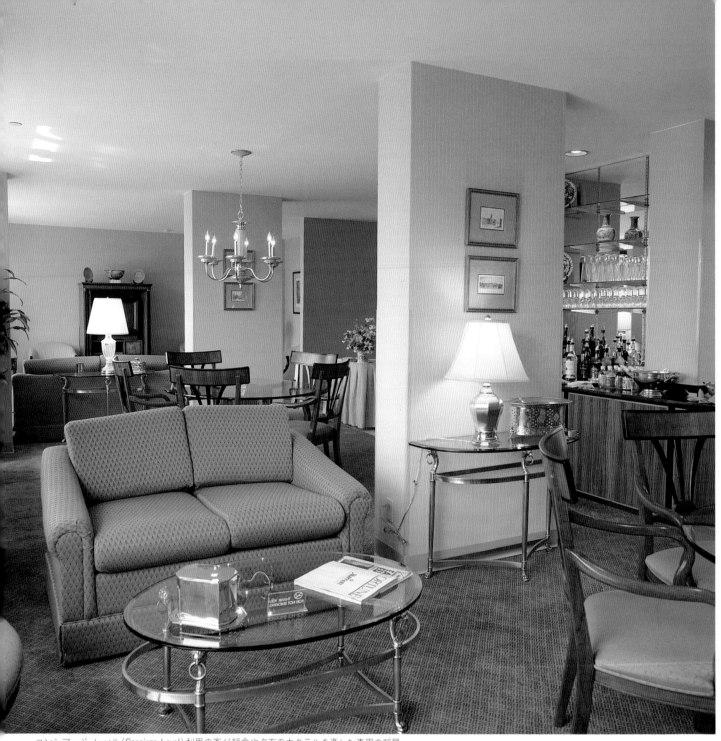

コンシアージ レベル(Concirge Level)利用の客が朝食や夕方のカクテルを楽しむ専用の部屋

The room exclusively used by guests occupying the "Concierge Level," to enjoy breakfast or cocktail in the evening.

大きなインドア スイミングプール

The large indoor swimming pool.

エクササイズ ルーム

The exercise room.

地上52階建て　638室の客室　コンファレンスセンター　ハドソンシアターなど3つのコンプレックスで構成されている

Having 52 stories above the ground, the hotel forms a complex of three facilities – hotel (638 rooms), conference center, and "Hudson Theatre."

Hotel Macklowe

145 West 44th Street New York, N. Y. 10036
Phone/212-768-4400

44th Street 側のエントランスのドアマン

The entrance on the 44th St. side.

モダンアートのあるエントランス

The entrance decorated with a modern art.

イタリアのアーチスト・Carlo Maria Mariani氏による“ナイト&ディ”と題する大きな絵は“男と女”を描き　ロビーの大きな壁面を占める

The large lobby wall is occupied with a large painting entitled "Night & Day" by Carlo Maria Mariani, an Italian artist, who intended to express "man and woman" in the painting.

エントランス ホールを通してラウンジとレストランをみる

The lounge and restaurant viewed across the entrance hall.

壁面前のレセプションとユニークなフロアデザイン

The reception and unique floor design before the wall.

大理石を使用したフロント レセプション

The reception accented with marble in a dignified manner.

ロビー ラウンジとバー
The lobby lounge and bar.

ホテル マックロウ

タイムス スクエア(Times Square)を中心とする再開発は約35億ドルを投じて進められ このホテルもそのプロジェクトのひとつである。44と45丁目(West 44 & 45th Street)にぬける1ブロックの一角に地上52階 638室のホテル棟を中心に38室の会議室を有する最新のビジネスタイプのホテルとして注目されている。利用客はビジネスマンたち いわゆるコーポレイト ピープルが60%を占め他はツーリストなど。オーナーのハリー マックロウ(Harry Macklowe)氏の精神がホテルの隅々にまで生かされ 利用客を満足させるための施設やサービス 従業員の対応に至るまでの配慮が素晴らしい。ホテル独自のMacktel Systemが新しいテレ コミュニケイションや情報として導入され TVモニターによる航空券の予約や変更 メッセージの受信 ルームサービスのオーダー ショッピングや劇場 ミュージアム スポーツ イベントなどの案内 ホテルの宿泊費の精算からチェックアウトまで客室に居ながらにして出来る。各部屋は自動空調で 100%コットンのシーツ 通話待ちの2台の電話(call waiting)やおつまみ付きの冷蔵庫などが設備されており人気が高い。

開　　　業:1990年5月
経　　　営:Hotel Macklowe Management Company
規模・客室数:地上52階 638室
料 飲 施 設:Lobby Bar & Lounge/Charlotte Restaurant(90席)
宴会・会議室:Macklowe Conference Center(100,000 Sq. feet)/ミーティングルーム(38)/Hudson Theatre(650名収容)
その他施設:ビジネスセンター/フィットネスセンター/ギフトショップ/Macktel System
デ ザ イ ン:建築/Perkins & Will, New York
内装/William Derman, A. I. A.

全体をアフリカン マホガニーで仕上げている
The interior is generally finished with African mahogany.

HOTEL MACKLOWE

With investments, totaling about $3,500 million, this area around Times Square has been subjected to redevelopment. Construction of this hotel has been completed as one of the projects. The "Hotel Macklowe" is drawing attention as the latest business type hotel situated at a corner of a block ranging from West 44th to 45th street; it has 638 guest rooms and 38 conference rooms on 52 stories above ground. 60% of its users are businessmen or so-called corporate people, and other users include tourists, etc. The management spirit of the owner Harry Macklowe permeates every nook and corner of the hotel, with wonderful considerations given to user satisfaction through attentive services and the hospitable attitude of employees. As a new telecommunication and information service means, the hotel's own "Macktel System" is introduced so that on a TV monitor guests can reserve or change aviation tickets, receive messages, order room service, be provided with information on museum or sporting events, or even receive a statement concerning hotel charges and checkout instructions while staying in their room. Rooms are very popular, since they are automatically air conditioned, and equipped with 100% cotton sheets, two call waiting telephones, a refrigerator which contains snacks, etc.

Opened : May 1990
Management : Hotel Macklowe Management Company
Scale · number of rooms : 52 stories above the ground; 638 rooms
Eating & drinking facilities : Lobby Bar & Lounge/ Charlotte Restaurant (90 seats)
Banquet & conference facilities: Macklowe Conference Center (100,000 Sq. feet)/ meeting rooms (38)/Hudson Theatre (accommodates 650 persons)
Other facilities: Business center/fitness center/ gift shop/Macktel System
Design : Architecture/Perkings & Will, New York
Interior/William Derman, A.I.A.

ロビー フロア　中央部にあるグランド ステア ケイスから見下ろすセキュリティとエレベーター ホール
The security and elevator hall overlooked from the grand staircase in the center of the lobby floor.

客室エレベーター ホール前にあるハウス ホーンを置いたテーブル
The table with a house phone in front of the guest room's elevator hall.

1902年に建てられたランドマーク「Hudson Theatre」のロビー
The lobby of "Hudson Theatre" which was built in 1902, and remains as a landmark.

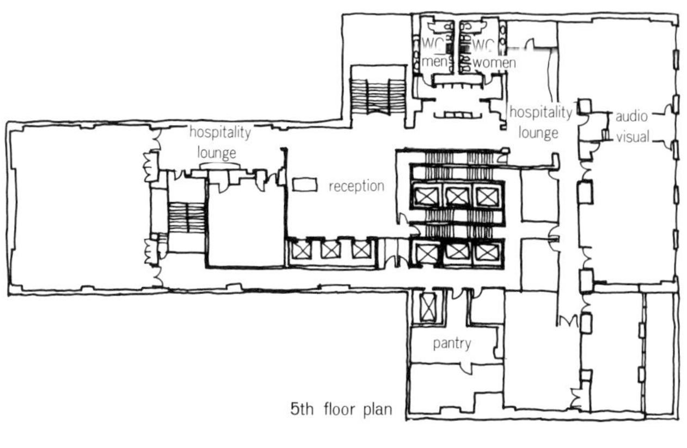

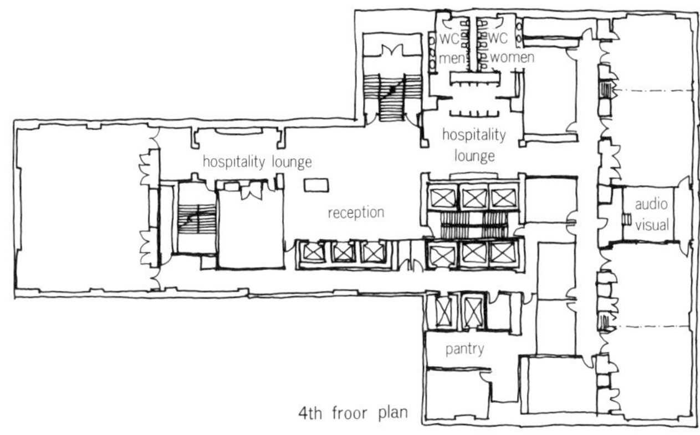

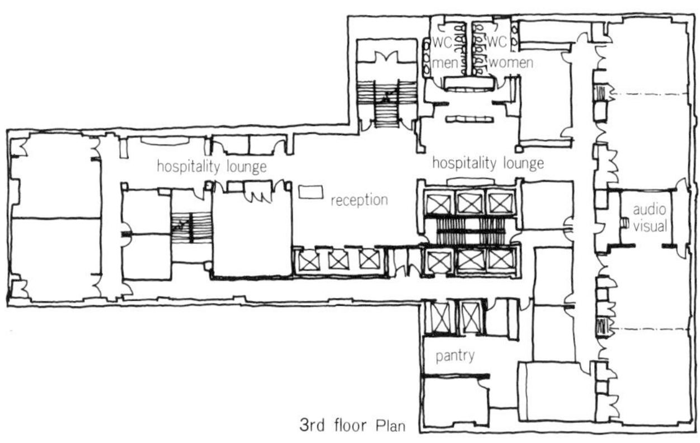

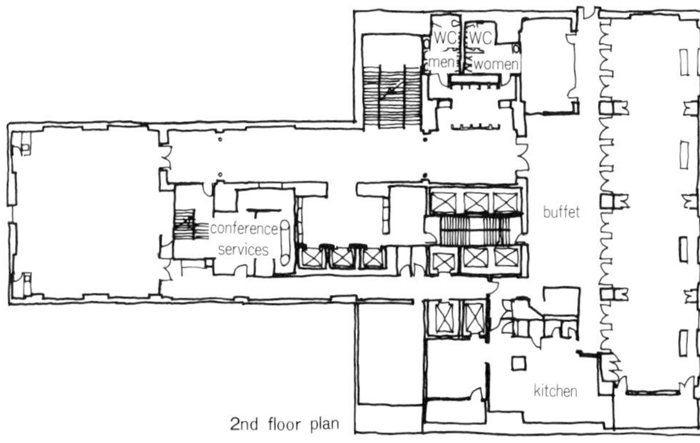

左上/エレベーター ホールと表示
左中/特長のある品揃えをしているギフトショップ
左下/フィットネス センター

Left, top / The elevator hall and display.
Left, center / The gift shop featuring a unique assortment of goods.
Left, bottom / The fitness center.

併設するコンファレンス センターのロビー　100,000Sq.Ft.の広さ　38室で構成されている
The lobby of the conference center annexed to the hotel; composed of 38 rooms using 100,000 sq. ft. of space.

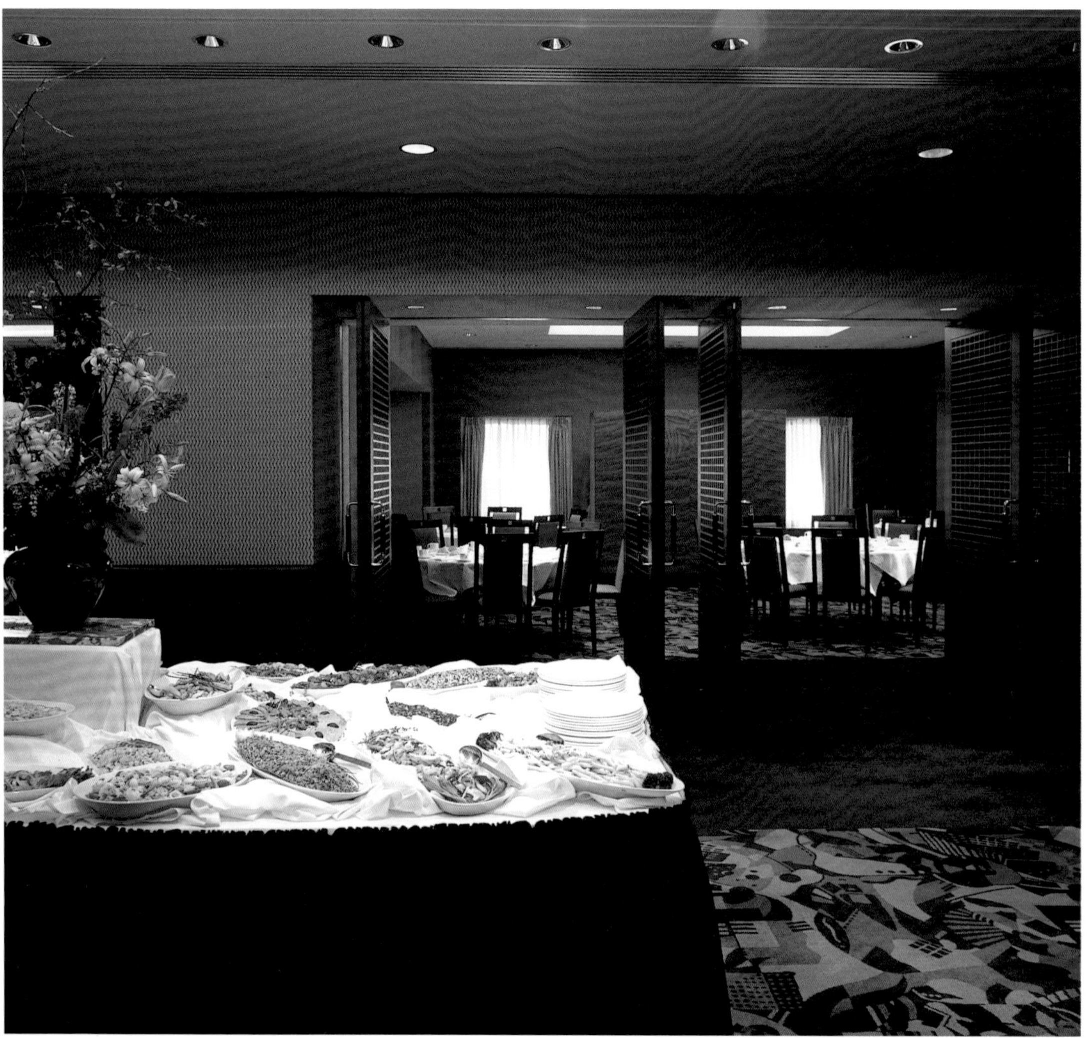

ビュッフェ式の食事をとりながら会議もできる
A conference can be held, side by side with buffet-style eating.

コンファレンス ダイニングと室外フロアのビュッフェをみる
The buffet utilizing the outdoor floor of the conference center.

オーディオ ビジュアル装置を備えた会議室 1時間に5回 部屋の空気が自動的に入れ替えられる
The conference room equipped with audiovisual units; room air is automatically ventilated 5 times an hour.

コンファレンス センターの室外フロアを利用したビュッフェ
The conference-dining space and the buffet on the outdoor floor.

小さなミーティングルーム 照明が上下 左右自由に移動できる
The small meeting room; lighting can be moved up and down, and right- and leftwards.

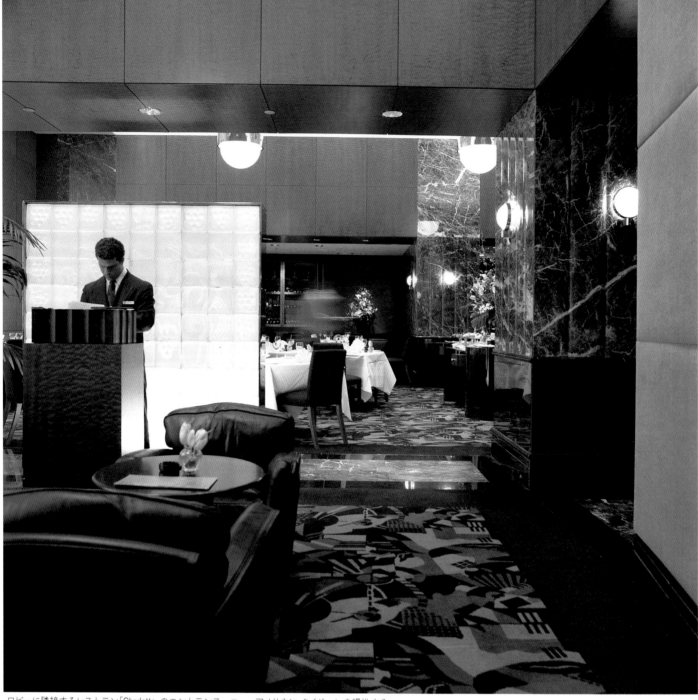

ロビーに隣接するレストラン「Charlotte」のエントランス　ニューアメリカン クイジーンを提供する
The entrance to the restaurant “Charlotte” adjoining the lobby; serves new American cuisine.

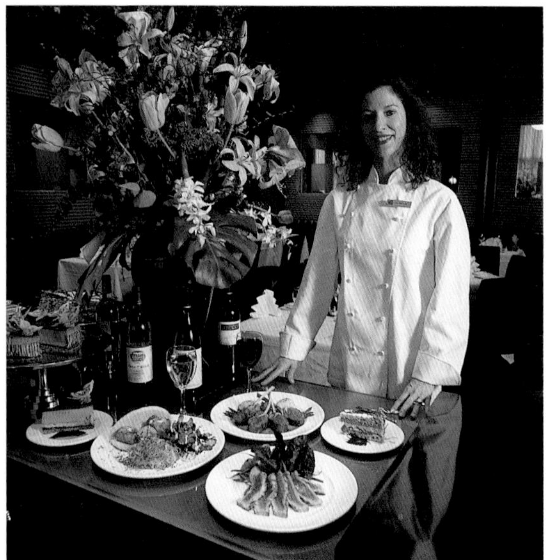

新しいアメリカ料理を開発するシェフのPatricia Willams さん
The chef Patricia Williams developing her cuisine.

ホームメードのデザートも好評
Homemade dessert is also popular.

高い天井　ユニークな照明　壁面のミラーなどポスト モダン感覚のレストラン
The high ceiling, unique lighting, mirror on the wall, etc. – the interior features these “postmodern” elements.

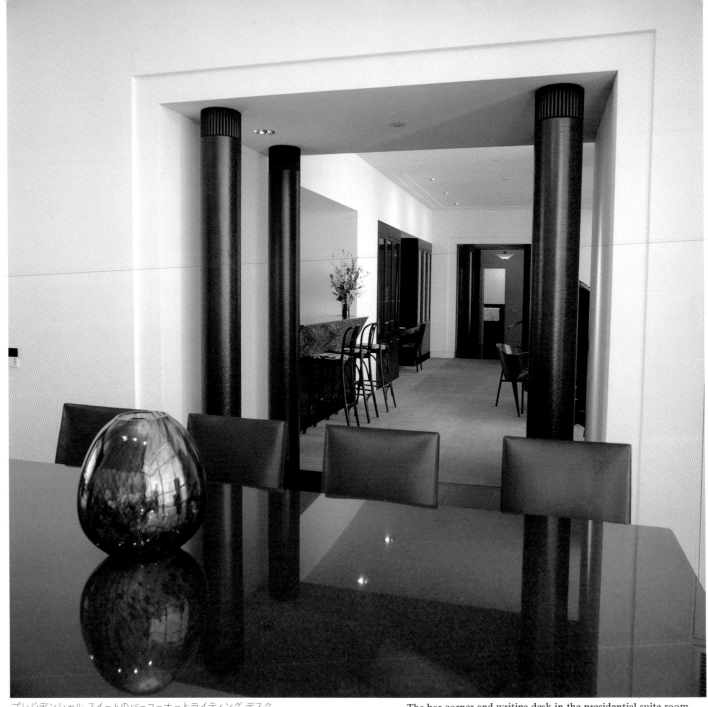

プレジデンシャル スイートのバーコーナーとライティング デスク

The bar corner and writing desk in the presidential suite room.

ツイン ルーム

The twin room.

マスターベッド ルーム

The master's bedroom.

スエードのソファや大きなTVセットを備えたリビングルーム　ウェット バーもみえる

The living room equipped with a suede sofa and large TV set; the wet bar is also visible.

ウェット バーからリビングルームをみる

The living room viewed from the wet bar.

白と黒の大理石を使用したバスルーム

The bathroom finished with black & white marble.

"ブロードウェイの一つのシンボル"として誕生したホテル　デザインはAlan Lapidus氏
The hotel designed by Alan Lapidus as a "symbol of Broadway."

地上46階建て　770室の外観
The appearance of the hotel having 770 rooms on 46 stories above the ground.

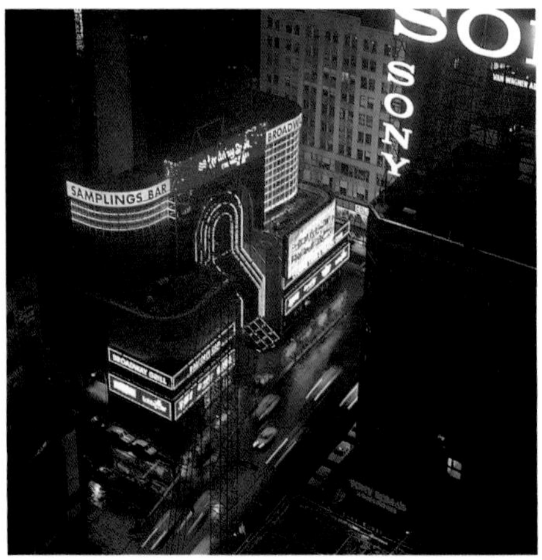

ブロードウェイに溶け込む夜のファサード
The facade at night fusing into the Broadway scenery.

1605 Broadway at 49th Street New York, N.Y. 10019
Phone/212-977-4000

高い天井空間のエスカレーターホール　ロビーと上階の宴会　会議室を結ぶ
The escalator hall under the high ceiling; connects the lobby with the upper banquet and conference rooms.

一段高くなったロビーの中央部　グリーンや花々がよりエレガントな雰囲気を演出している

The central part of the lobby which is a little higher than the surrounding parts; presenting a more elegant atmosphere with greenery and flowers.

ゲストサービス デスクとフロントをみる

The guest service desk and front.

朝食もサービスするロビーバー

The lobby bar which also serves breakfast.

エスカレーター ホールを通してブロードウェイ通りの「Sampling Bar」をみる
The sampling bar facing the Broadway viewed across the escalator hall.

大理石を使用した重厚な雰囲気のレセプション
The front reception using marble.

ホリデイ イン クラウン プラザ

1952年 テネシー州メンフィス(Memphis)に一つのモーターロッジが生まれたのが 今日の世界最大のホテルチェーンを誇る「ホリディ イン」の出発であった。以来約40年間の歴史はアメリカのホテルチェーンの歴史であり 幾多の変化や進歩が見られる。無料テレビやベッドサイドに置く電話機 フリーアイス プール施設などの標準化に始まり 予約のコンピューター化 ケーブルテレビ サテライト通信によるテレビ会議の導入など 近代テクノロジーの発展と共に このホテルチェーンはいち早く取り入れている。

ニューヨークのシアター街の中心地に新装なったこの「クラウン プラザ」は 従来の施設を更にグレードアップしたもので 設計の建築家 Alan Lapidus氏が云うように"ブロードウェイの一つのシーン(scene)になるようデザインしたホテル＝The hotel is definitely designed to be part of the Broadway scene"として誕生した。ブロードウェイ通り(Broadway Avenue)に面した外観は 点滅するネオンとイルミネーション 連なるボールライトなどが交差し まさにブロードウェイのシーンの中に溶け込み 人と建物が一体となったとき何かエキサイティングな雰囲気を感じさせる。

競争の激しいニューヨークのホテル業界にあって このホテルでは質とサービスを重んじている。"従業員教育に多くの時間とエネルギーを費やし 彼等のミステイクを恐れず 信頼し励ますことにより 素晴らしい人材が育つと信じる"とマネージング ディレクターの Michael Silberstein 氏は云う。このように素晴らしい建物とスタッフたちによって築かれる高度のイメージアップが 一層求められている時代といえる。

開　　業：1989年12月1日
規模・客室数：地上46階 770室(内 キング レジャールーム279室 クイーンルーム83室 スタンダード ルーム231室 ハンディキャップ用ルーム15室 エグゼクティブフロアー(最上の4フロアー)113室 スイートルーム3室 等を含む)
クラウン プラザ クラブ(46階)
料 飲 施 設：18,000Sq, feet 大宴会場(700名収容)/会議・宴会場23
その他施設：ヘルス クラブ(8,800Sq, feet)/50フィート インドアプール/サウナ

HOLIDAY INN CROWNE PLAZA

In 1952 a motor lodge appeared in Memphis, Tennessee. It was the starting point of "Holiday Inn" which is currently the world's largest hotel chain. Its history for the subsequent 40 years has also been a history of hotels in America which have undergone various changes while making progress. Starting with the standardization of free TV service, bedside telephones, free ice, pool facilities, etc., the hotel chain has introduced various service means such as a computerized reservation systems, cable TV and TV conferences through satellite communications; all of which have been made possible along with modern technological progress.

The "Crowne Plaza" was born in the central part of a theater street in New York, with more upgraded equipment than in conventional hotels of the chain. Alan Lapidus, the architect who undertook the architectural design, rightly said: "The hotel is definitely designed to be part of the Broadway scene." Facing Broadway Avenue, the facade just melts into the Broadway scene with its blinking neons, illumination, ball lights, etc. When people become one with the building, a somewhat exciting atmosphere can be felt.

Amidst the very competitive hotel business in New York, the "Crowne Plaza" emphasizes quality and service. "We believe that by spending much time and energy in employee training, and relying on and encouraging them without worrying if they might commit a mistake, wonderful staff can be nurtured," says Mr. Michael Silberstein, managing director. It may be said that now is the time when a higher hotel image can be created through both a wonderful building and staff.

Opened : December 1, 1989
Scale · number of guest rooms: 46 stories above the ground; 770 rooms (king leisure rooms 279, queen rooms 83, standard rooms 231, rooms for the handicapped 15, rooms on executive floors (4 top floors) 113, suite rooms 3, etc.), as well as the Crowne Plaza Club (46th floor)
Eating & drinking facilities: The Balcony Cafe (Buffet – 136 seats)/ Sampling Bar (145 seats), Lobby Bar/Broadway Grill (120 seats)
Banquet & conference facilities: 18,000 sq. feet, Large banquet hall (accommodates 700 persons)/Conference . banquet hall – 23)
Other facilities: Health club (8,800 sq. feet)/50-feet indoor pool/ sauna

タイムズ スクエアに面したバーラウンジ「Sampling Bar」

The sampling bar on the bar lounge facing the Times Square.

エントランスからバーカウンターをみる

The bar counter viewed from the entrance.

「The Balcony Cafe」のビュッフェコーナー

The buffet corner of "The Balcony Cafe."

朝　昼　夕とビュッフェスタイルを中心に食事を提供する「The Balcony Cafe」のダイニング エリア
The dining area in "The Balcony Cafe" serves foods in the morning, at noon and in the evening, mainly in buffet style.

700名収容のボール ルーム　他に23のミーティング ルームがある　The ballroom capable of accommodating 700 persons; there also are 23 meeting rooms.

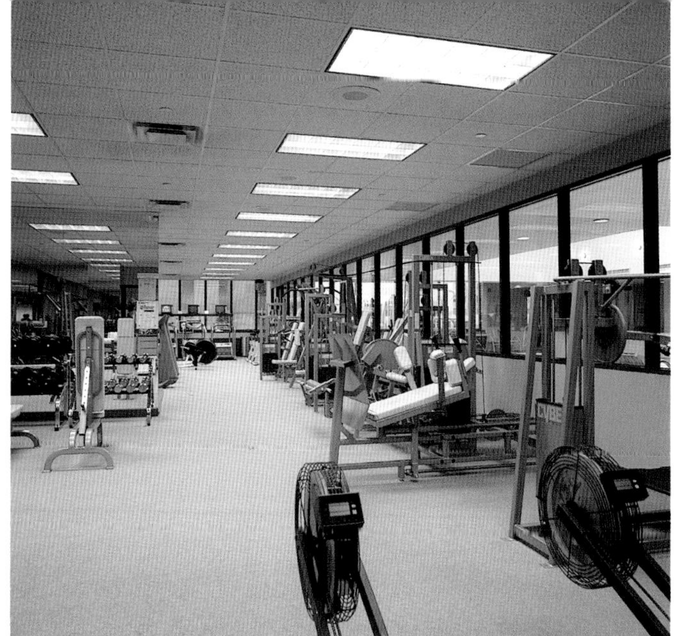

ホテルのヘルス クラブとしてはN.Y.でも最大クラス
One of the largest health clubs attached to hotels in New York.

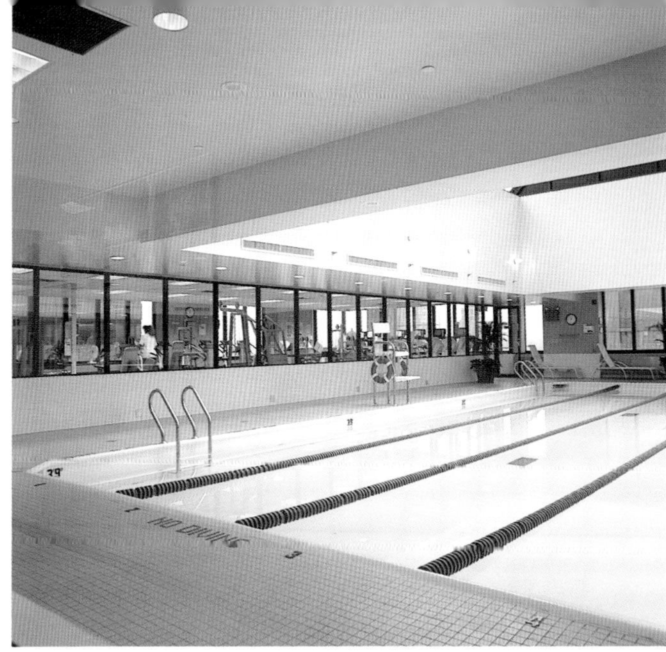

50フィートのスイミング プール
The 50-feet swimming pool.

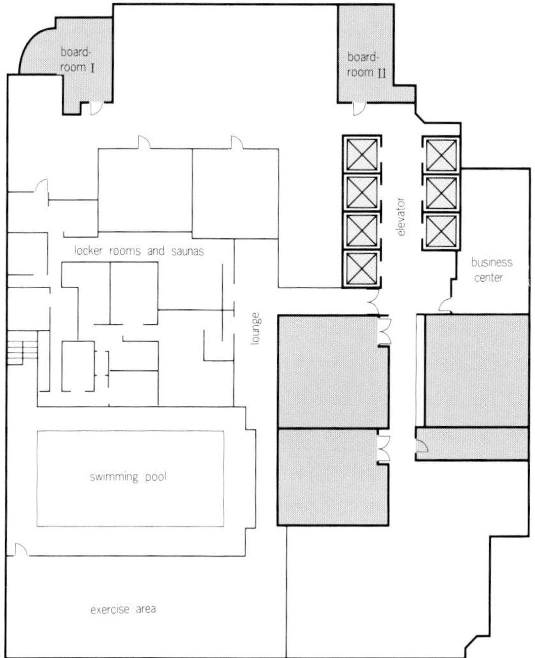

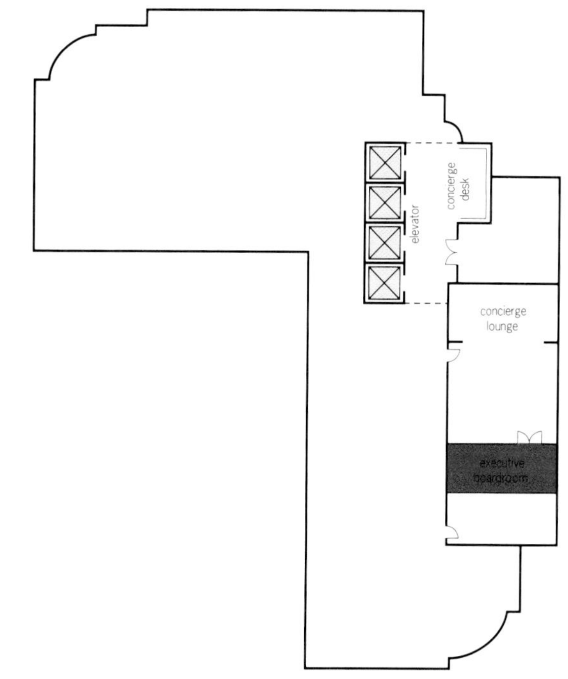

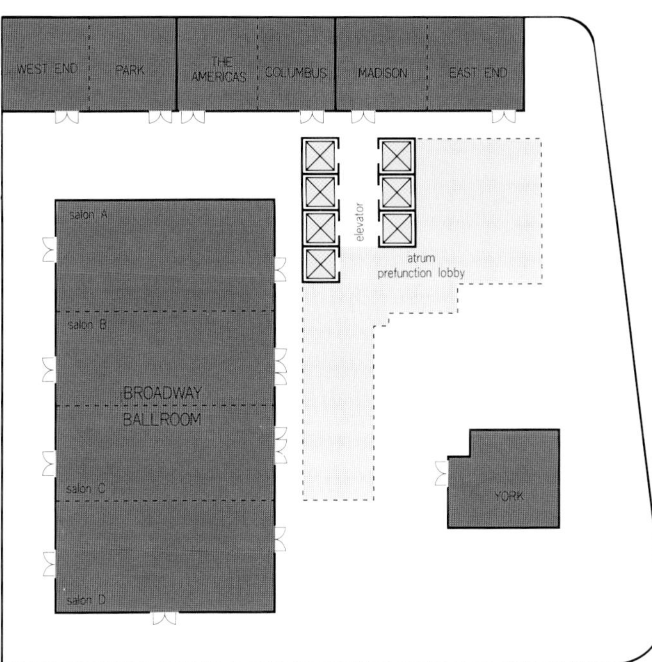

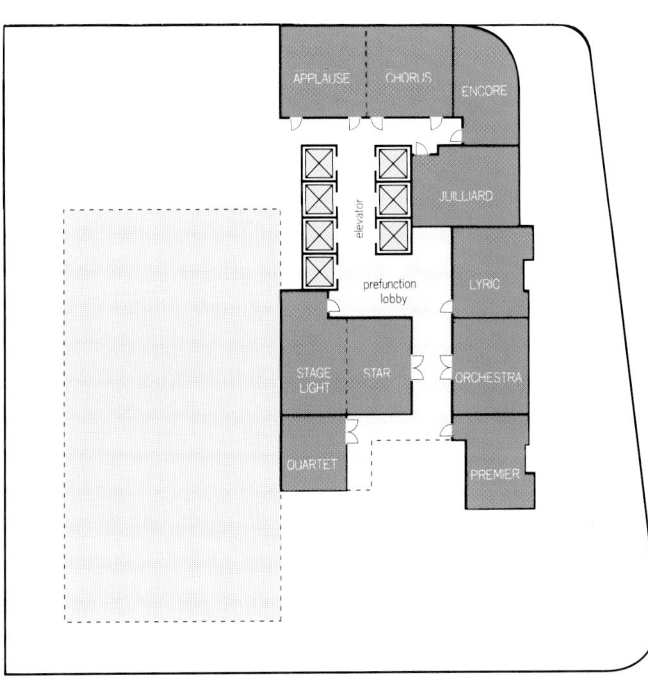

最上階にあるクラウン プラザ クラブのゲストが利用するラウンジ
The lounge used by guests to the Crowne Plaza Club on the highest floor.

クラブのゲストのためのコンシアージ サービス デスク 113室と3つのスイートを管理する
The concierge service desk for guests to the club; controlling 113 rooms and 3 suite rooms.

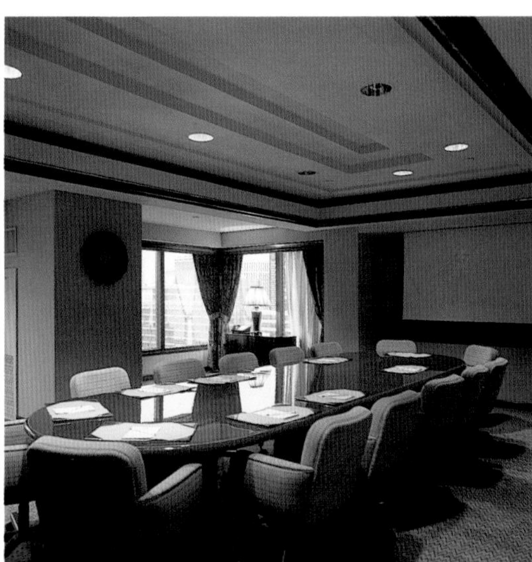

エグゼクティブ ボードルームはクラブ メンバーのみが利用できる部屋
The executive boardroom can be used only by the club members.

クラブ メンバーが利用するプライベート ラウンジ　朝食と夕方のカクテルやオードブルを提供する
The private lounge used by the club members; serves morning and evening cocktails and hors d'œuvre.

プレジデンシャル スイートのリビング ルーム

The living room in the presidential suite room.

クイーン サイズのベッドと暖かな雰囲気のあるツインのゲストルーム

The twin guest room having a queen-sized bed and warm atmosphere.

VIP客に対するホテル側からのもてなし

The hotel staff entertaining the VIPs.

約30年ぶりにリノベーションなったロビー　重厚のなかにもカジュアルさを加えている
The lobby renewed after about 30 years; puts on a dignified but casual appearance.

ホテルのメイン エントランスに隣接するレストランのファサード
The facade of the restaurant adjoining the hotel's main entrance.

2600万ドルを投じてリノベーションした729室のホテル
The hotel with 729 rooms redecorated by investing $26 million.

569 Lexington Avenue at 51st Street New York, N.Y. 10022
Phone/212-752-7000

広い空間のレセプション廻り

The spacious reception area.

ロビー ラウンジからレセプション方向をみる

The reception area viewed from the lobby lounge.

建築家・Peter Nemietz 氏がデザインした1940年代のモダン アート スタイルのレストラン・Lexington Avenue Grill（250席）
"Lexington Avenue Grill" (250 seats), a restaurant in the 1940s modern art style designed by architect Peter Nemietz.

大きな壁面にはホテルの歴史と時代に話題となった人やテーマが描かれていて興味深い
On the large wall the history of the hotel, and persons and topics hotly talked about in each age are painted, arousing much interest.

ロビー前のバーコーナー
The bar corner in front of the lobby.

ロウズ サミット ホテル

ロウズ ホテルズはアメリカ カナダ モナコに15軒展開し 全客室数7,291室の中規模ホテルチェーンである。中でもニューヨークの「ロウズ サミット ホテル」は 1961年にオープンしたグループ中最古のホテルであり 第二次世界大戦後ニューヨークに建てられた最初のホテルとしても有名で アイゼンハワー元大統領もプレジデンシャル スイートルームに泊まっている。1991年の7月で30周年を迎えるにあたって 約3年間を費やし 宴会 会議室とゲストルームに2,100万ドル ロビーやレストランに500万ドルを投じ 大がかりなリノベーションを終えたところだ。766室あった客室を729室に減らし 各部屋の面積を広くとり 新たに4室のエグゼクティブ スイート(jucuzzi付き)と 33室のジュニア スイートを加えている。過去18年間に渡って"USオープンテニス"のオフィシャル ホテルとして利用されてきたのをはじめ アンパイアーやスキーチーム 体操 フットボール 野球の選手など スポーツ関係者の利用が多いことでも有名で そのためにフィットネスセンターのサイズを倍にするなどの配慮もしている。もう一つのハイライトは ロビーに隣接する「Lexington Avenue Grill」レストランで 建築家・Peter Nemietz氏のデザインの1940年代のモダーンアート スタイル。大きな壁画にはホテルの歴史と その時代の話題となる人物などが描かれていて興味深い。日替わりメニューやアメリカの地方料理(American regional cuisine)が売りものである。

開　　　業:1991年(リニューアル)
規模・客室数:729室
料 飲 施 設:Lexington Avenue Grill/Lobby Bar
宴会・会議室:12,000 Sq. feet 12室(最大450名収容)
その他施設:ヘルス クラブ/ドラッグ&ニューズスタンド/理容室

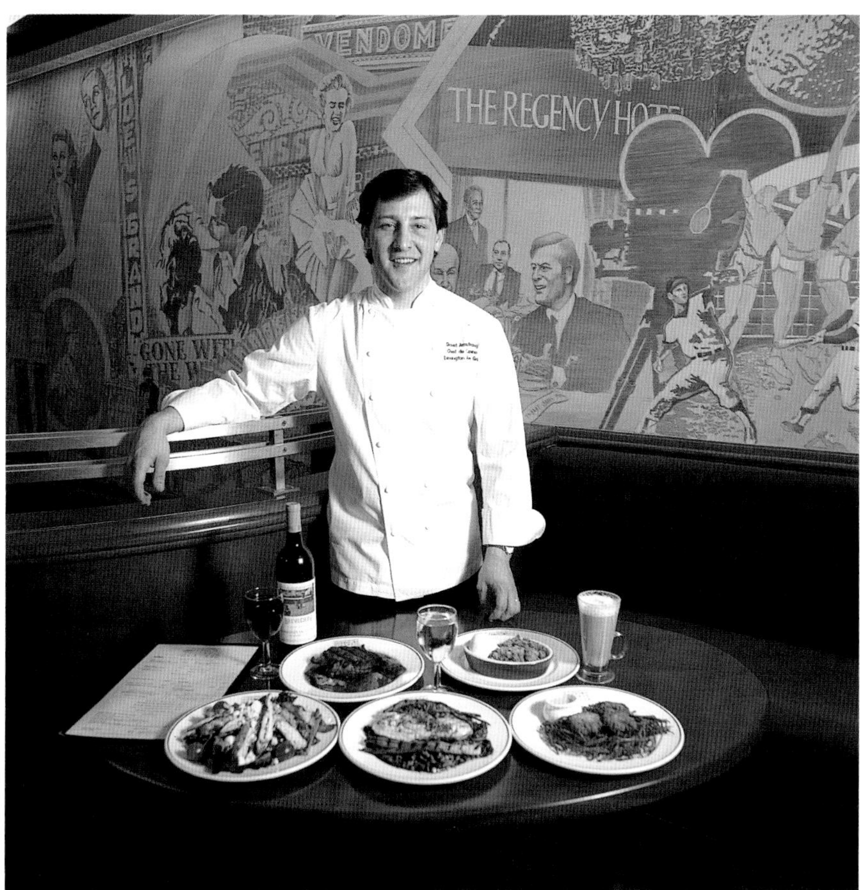

'90年代の料理(the cuisine of the '90s)を提供するシェフのDavid Armstrong氏
The chef David Armstrong who offers the cuisine of the '90s.

LOEWS SUMMIT HOTEL

Having 15 hotels in America, Canada and Monaco, the "Loews Hotel" chain is a medium-scale hotel chain having 7,291 rooms in total. Opened in 1961, "Loews Summit Hotel" is the oldest in the group, and also known as the first hotel built in New York after the Second World War. The former President Eisenhower also stayed in the Presidential Suite Room. On the occasion of the 30th anniversary in July 1991, the hotel has completed an extensive renovation by spending about 3 years, with a $21 million investment for banquet halls, conference rooms and guest rooms, and $5 million for lobbies and restaurants. By reducing the number of guest rooms from 766 to 729, the space for each room has been increased, while 4 executive suite rooms (with jacuzzi) and 33 junior suite rooms have been newly added. For the last 18 years the "Loews Summit Hotel" has been used as an official hotel for the "US Open Tennis Championships," and is also known widely for being used by many people involved in sports, including umpires, ski team members, gymnasts, football, baseball and other players. To satisfy them, the hotel has doubled the fitness center's size. Another highlight is the restaurant "Lexington Avenue Grill" adjacent to the lobby – it is built in the modern art style of the 1940's designed by architect Peter Nemietz. On the large wall the history of the hotel, topical persons of each age, etc. are painted, arousing much interest. The restaurant features a menu whose items change day to day, centering around American regional cuisine.

Opened : 1991 (renewal)
Scale · number of rooms: 729 rooms
Eating & drinking facilities: Lexington Avenue Grill/Lobby Bar
Banquet & conference facilities: 12,000 sq. feet 12 rooms (maximum accommodates 450 persons)
Oather facilities: Health club/drug & newsstand/hairdressing saloon

新しく加えられたエグゼクティブ スイート ルーム

The newly added "executive suite" room.

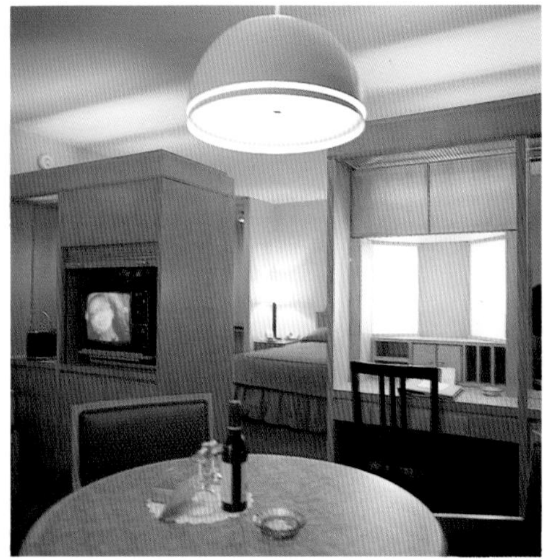

ジュニア スイート ルーム

The "junior suite" room.

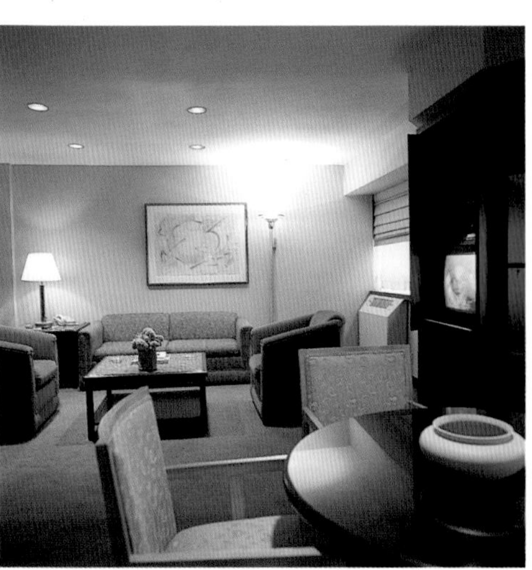

スペースも広くなったスイート ルームのリビング

The suite room's living room which has become more spacious than before.

大きなミラーのライティング デスクは部屋の広がりをみせている

The room looks very spacious due to lighting using a large mirror.

キングサイズのマスター ベッドルーム

The king-sized master's bedroom.

大きなジャグジーがあるバスルーム

The bathroom with a large Jacuzzi.

ペントハウスの宴会　会議室はプレジデンタルルームとサミット コンチネンタル ルームで構成されている
Banqueting on the penthouse; conference rooms are composed of presidential and summit continental rooms.

ディナーのテーブル セッティング
The dinner table setting.

朝食ミーティング用にセットされた天窓付会議室
The conference room with a skylight set for a breakfast meeting.

VIP用フロア(17階)/ESPレベルのラウンジ

The (17th) floor for VIPs/lounge on the ESP level.

AV装置完備の会議室"Addabbo"

The conference room "ADDABBO" fully equipped with audiovisual units.

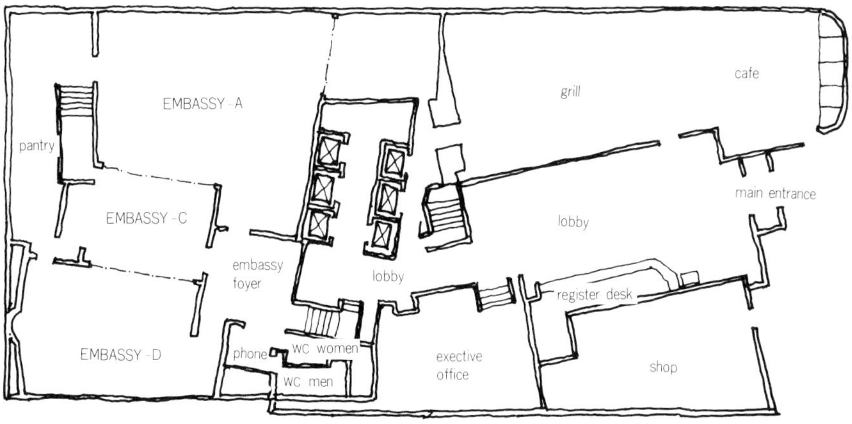

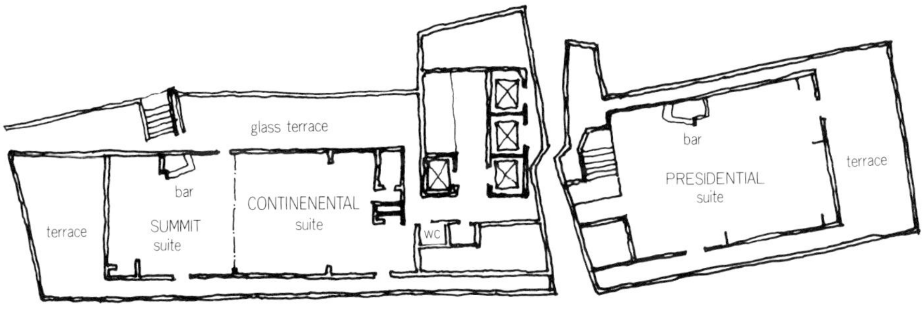

EMBASSY-A
pantry
EMBASSY-C
EMBASSY-D
embassy foyer
phone
WC women
WC men
lobby
grill
cafe
main entrance
lobby
register desk
exective office
shop

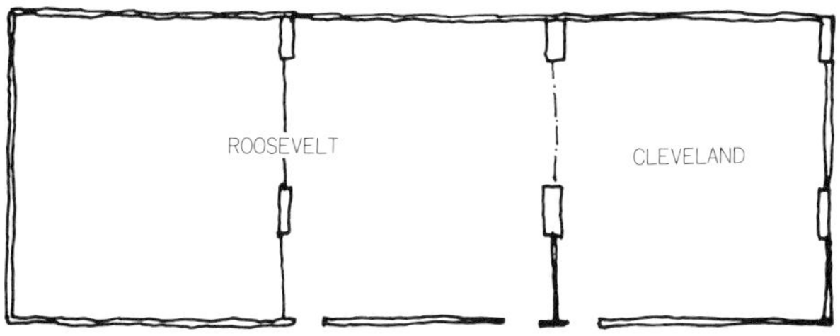

ROOSEVELT
CLEVELAND

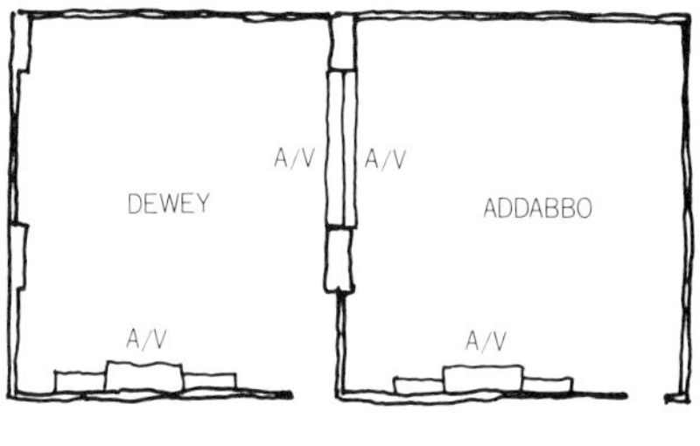

DEWEY
A/V
A/V
ADDABBO
A/V
A/V

glass terrace
terrace
bar
SUMMIT suite
CONTINENENTAL suite
WC
bar
PRESIDENTIAL suite
terrace

カラフルなエレベーター ホール フロア毎に色を変えている

The colorful elevator hall; each floor is differently colored.

スポーツ関係の宿泊者が多いため このフィットネス センターも2倍に増床した

Since the hotel is used by many people who are related to sports, the fitness center space has been doubled.

ロビー　既存ビル(6階)の上に33階のホテルを建てたため　ホテルの基礎部分をミラーで覆いかくしている
The lobby; since the 33-storied hotel has been constructed on the existing building (6-storied), the hotel's foundation is covered up with a mirror.

Hotel
novotel

226 West 52nd Street on Broadway New York, N. Y. 10019-5804
Phone/212-315-0100

ホテルのエントランスは専用エレベーターで上り7階にある
One uses an exclusive elevator to access the hotel's entrance which is on the 7th floor.

ホテルは7階から33階部分を使用している
The 7th to 33rd floors are used by the hotel.

ロビーを通してレストラン方向をみる

The restaurant area viewed across the lobby.

レセプション　横にみえるワゴンは忙しいビジネス客のために朝のコーヒーを無料でサービスするためのもの

The reception; the wagon beside the reception is used to serve busy business guests with morning coffee free of charge.

ロビーに隣接するギフトショップ

The gift shop adjoining the lobby.

天井をミラーとステンレスで仕上げたロビー　The lobby whose ceiling is finished with a mirror and stainless steel.

バーカウンターからラウンジとロビーをみる

The lounge and lobby viewed from the bar counter.

ノボテル ニューヨーク

フランスを中心に世界の50ヶ国に280軒以上のホテルを展開しているこの「ノボテル」は "ザ ユーロピアン タッチ(The European Touch)"をキャッチフレーズにし 主にビジネス客を対象にした経済的なホテル。北アメリカとカナダに9軒が進出している。このニューヨークのブロードウェイに面したホテルの建物は 6階までが古くからあったオフィスビルで 7階から上がホテルとして増築されたもの。したがってホテル専用エレベーターは7階(ロビー)以上からとなっている。ロビー階はレストランとバーラウンジとで大部分を占め 会議室が2部屋あるだけで 他は客室ばかりで構成された宿泊をメインにしたホテルである。セキュリティには特に力を入れ ルームキーは電子ロック システムを採用するなど 女性の一人客でも 安心して泊まれる。客室やパブリックエリアには ヨーロッパのタッチが感じられる色使いや飾りがみられる。

開　　　業:1984年10月
規模・客室数:地上33階 474室
料 飲 施 設:Cafe Nicole Restaurant & Lounge

NOVOTEL NEW YORK

Operating more than 280 chain hotels in 50 countries centering around France, the "Novotel" employs "The European Touch" as a catch-phrase, and as an economical hotel it is mainly intended for business people. At present, there are 9 hotels in North America and Canada. The building now used by the hotel had been an old 6-storied office building, and the 7th and higher floors have been added for hotel use. An elevator exclusively for hotel use leads to the 7th floor's lobby. The lobby is spaciously occupied by a restaurant and bar lounge. Apart from only 2 conference rooms, all others are guest rooms. Thus, the hotel is mainly intended for those who wish to pass the night. Special considerations are given to security by employing an electronic locking system for each room key so that even a single female guest can stay and be at ease. The guest rooms and public areas are accented with coloring and decorations which make one feel the European touch.

Opened : October 1984
Scale · number of rooms: 33 stories above the ground; 474 rooms
Eating & drinking facilities: Cafe Nicole Restaurant & Lounge

サンルームスタイルのCafe Nicole　このカフェからみるタイムズスクェアの夜景は美しく好評だ　外側にはカフェテラスも設けている
The sunroom-styled cafe "NICOLE"; a view of the Times Square commanded from the cafe is beautiful and well received; on the outside there is a cafe terrace.

ヨーロピアンタッチの朝食ビュッフェが楽しめる

One can enjoy breakfast in the European style.

カフェの入口　右側に客室エレベーターへの通路がみえる

The entrance to the cafe; on the right side there is an aisle leading to elevators for guest rooms.

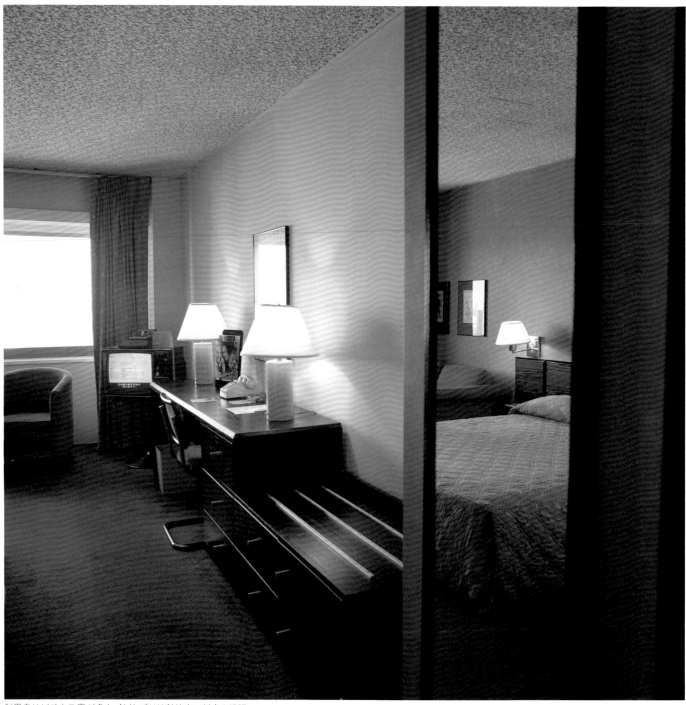

利用者はビジネス客が多く　N.Y.では比較的安い料金も好評
The hotel is used by many business guests, and its rates relatively low in New York are well received.

キングサイズの客室
The king-sized guest room.

中2階にあるミーティングルーム
The meeting room on the mezzanine.

N.Y.で最も高層のホテル(610フィート) また全室スイート型の高級ホテルとして話題になっている

The highest (610 feet) hotel in New York, "RIHGA ROYAL HOTEL" is also drawing attention as a high-class hotel entirely composed of suite rooms.

RIHGA ROYAL HOTEL
NEW YORK

151 West 54th Street New York, N. Y. 10019
Phone/212-307-5000

エントランス前に立つドアマン

The doorman standing in front of the entrance.

1920～30年代　パーク アベニューの住宅によく見られたロビーの雰囲気をデザイン　椅子は20世紀初期のホフマン スタイルで　その周りに3つの八角形のじゅうたんが敷かれている

An atmosphere of lobbies which were often seen in residences on the Park Avenue in the 1920s to 1930s was incorporated into the design; chairs are made in Hoffmann style early in the 20th century, surrounded with three sheets of octagonal carpet.

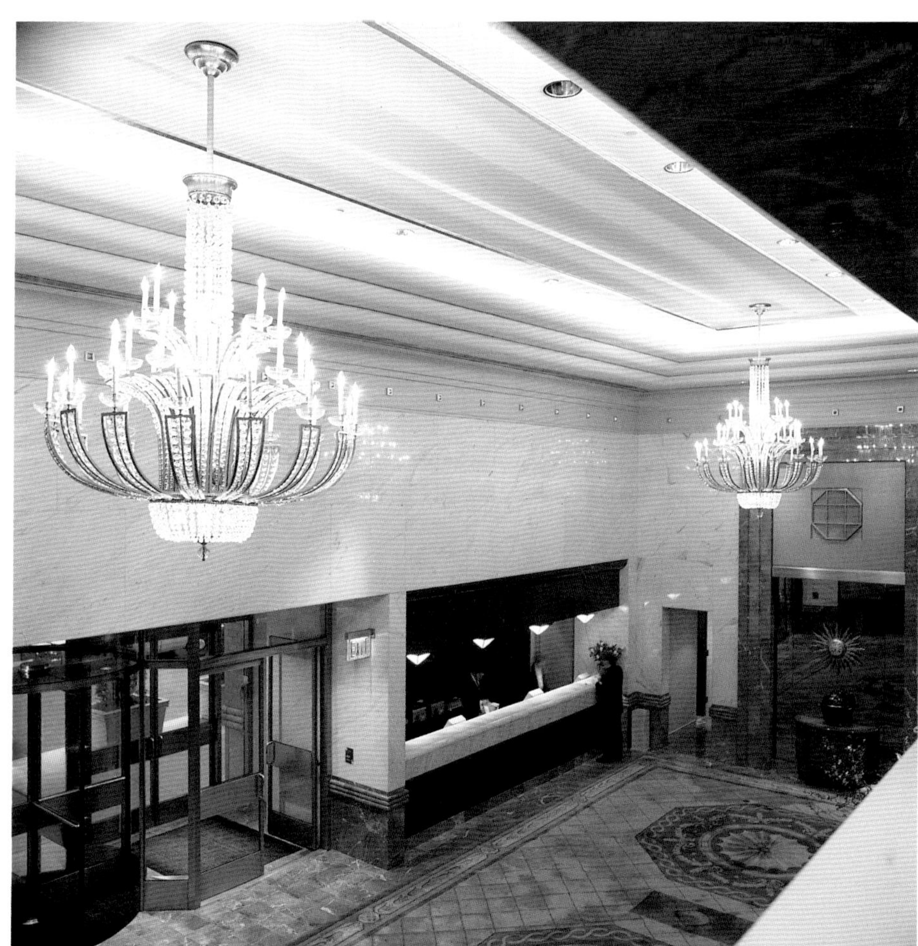

カスタム デザインのシャンデリアを通してエントランスとレセプションを見下す

The entrance and reception overlooked across the custom-designed chandeliers.

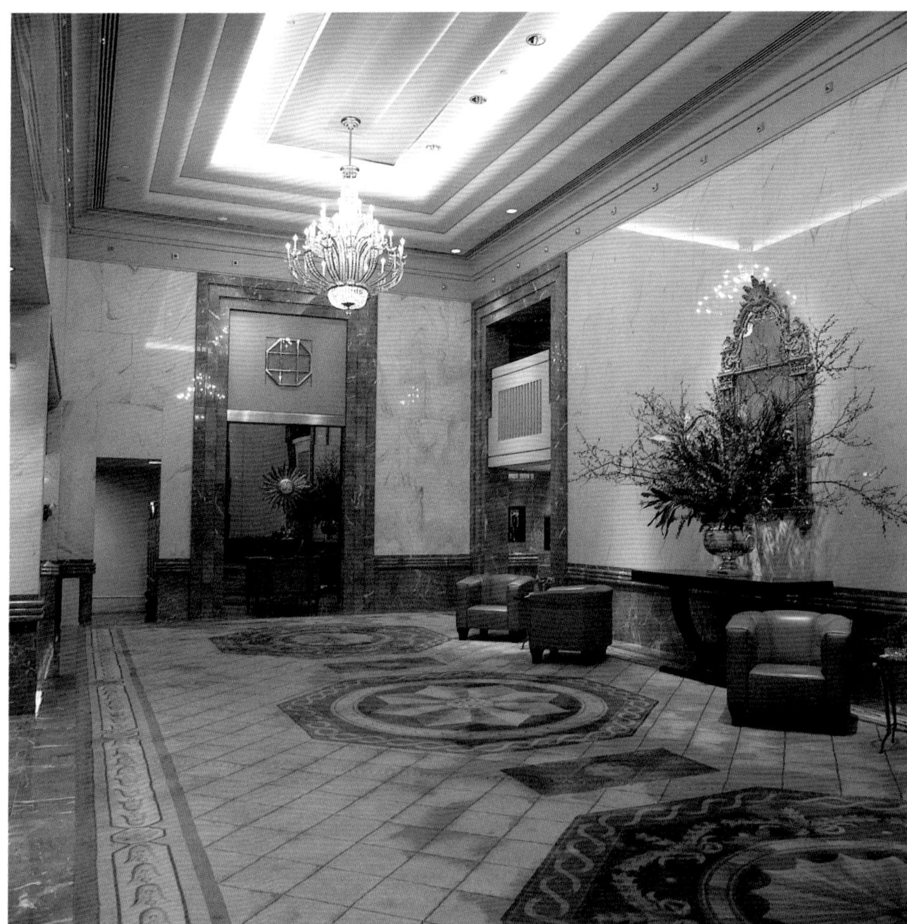

ロビーの中央には18世紀のフレンチ リージェンシィのミラーや1930年代のフレンチ コンソール テーブルが置かれている

In the center of the lobby, French regency mirror in the 18th century, French console table in the 1930s, etc. are placed.

ロビー ラウンジの入口あたりからバーコーナーをみる アフリカン マホガニーを使用した落ち着きのある雰囲気
The bar corner viewed from the entrance to the lobby lounge; presents a composed atmosphere due to the use of American mahogany.

リーガ ロイヤル ホテル

大阪のロイヤルホテルが出資する Rihga International U.S.A.Inc.の経営するオールスイート型 高級ホテル。外観は1920～30年代の摩天楼を思わせるクラシックなフォルムのベイ ウインド(Bay Windows)を配した610フィート(約183m)の高層ビルで ホテルとしてはニューヨークで最も高い建物である。500室のスイートはベッドルームとリビングルームがそれぞれ独立し ワン ベッドルームが572 sq, feet(53㎡―1泊260～390ドル) トゥーベッドルームが720sq, feet(67㎡―1泊450～700ドル)とかなりデラックスな感がある。室内の家具類はカスタム デザインで ピーチとティール(teal)カラーを主に使用している。各リビングルームは8名までの会合が可能で プライベイトな商談や会食が自分の部屋で出来るという便利さが売りもの。少々割高の部屋代も多目的に利用できて ビジネスマンたちの間では人気が高い。トップフロアーの53～54階に宴会及び会議室を設けているのも ホテルとして新しい試みである。ここからはマンハッタンのスカイラインやハドソン川 セントラルパーク イーストリバーなど 360度のパノラマが楽しめる。これらの素晴らしい眺望をセールスポイントの1つにし 他店との差別化を計り 従来のホテルとは異なるアップグレードなコンセプトを生み出し ニューヨークのホテル業界に新たな話題を提供し注目されている。

開　　業:1990年5月
規模・客室数:地上54階 500室
料 飲 施 設:Bar & Entertainment Lounge/Hal Restaurant(167席)
宴会・会議室:11室(2階 53～54階)
その他施設:ビジネスセンター/フィットネスセンター

RIHGA ROYAL HOTEL

An all suite type high class hotel operated by Rihga International U.S.A. Inc. in which the Royal Hotel in Osaka has invested. Its building is the highest in New York – 610 feet (about 183 m) – reminding us of a skyscraper from the 1920s to 1930s with classic bay windows. Each of the 500 suite rooms features an independent bedroom and living room, and one bedroom is 572 sq. feet (53 m^2 – \$260 to \$390 for a night's stay) and two bedrooms are 720 sq. feet (67 m^2 – \$450 to \$700 for a night's stay), thus offering a somewhat deluxe space. The interior pieces of furniture are custom-designed, and mainly use peach and teal colors. Since each living room can be put to various uses – for a meeting of up to 8 persons to have either private business talks or dine together, etc. – it is very popular with businessmen despite the somewhat costly room charges. One of the fresh moves of the hotel is the installation of banquet and conference rooms on the top 53rd and 54th floors, from which one can enjoy a commanding 360-degree panorama of Manhattan's skyline, River Hudson, Central Park, East River, etc. Using these wonderful views as one of its sales points and thereby creating an upscale image, the hotel has differentiated itself from its competitors and is being hotly talked about in the hotel business in New York.

Opened : May 1990
Scale · number of rooms: 54 stories above the ground; 500 rooms
Eating & drinking facilities: Bar & Entertainment Lounge/
Hal Restaurant (167 seats)
Banquet & conference facilities: 11 rooms (2nd floor and 53th to 54th floors)
Other facilities: Business center/fitness center

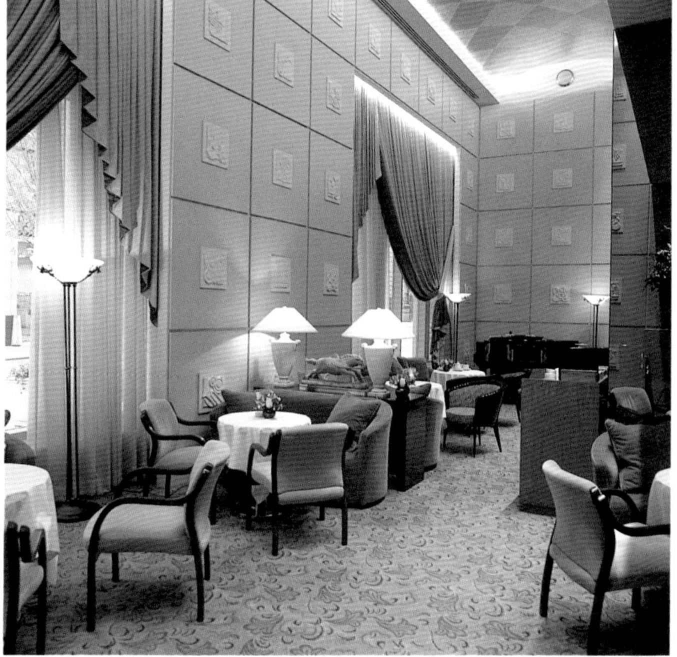

上/ロビー ラウンジ　カーテンはシルクを使用している
下/20フィートの天井高に金と銀のまだらのパターンを配し 四角いパネルには寓話像と幾何学模様のレリーフを施している

Top / The lobby lounge curtain uses silk.
Bottom / The ceiling 20 feet high features a pattern of gold & silver spots, and the square panels are embossed with fable images and geometrical patterns.

メイン ダイニングルーム・Halcyon(ハルシオン)120席　冬至ごろ海に巣を浮べ孵(ふ)卵中　波を静める魔力があると信じられている鳥の名に由来　静かで平和を意味する
The main dining room "HALCYON" with 120 seats; meaning quietness and peace, "halcyone" is the name of a bird which is believed to float its nest on the sea around the winter solstice, and can calm waves while warming the eggs.

レストラン入口のロータンダ

The rotunda by the entrance to the restaurant.

ヨーロッパに対抗し アメリカ人シェフが新しく作りあげ 組立てていく"ヌーボー アメリカン キュイジーン"を目指すエグゼクティブ シェフのJohn A. Halligan氏

The executive chef John A. Halligan who, as an American chef in rivalry with Europe, is challenging the creation of "nouveau American cuisine."

最上階の53～54階に設けたミーティングとバンケットのフロアを結ぶ階段廻り

The staircase area connecting the meeting and banquet areas on the highest 53rd and 54th floors.

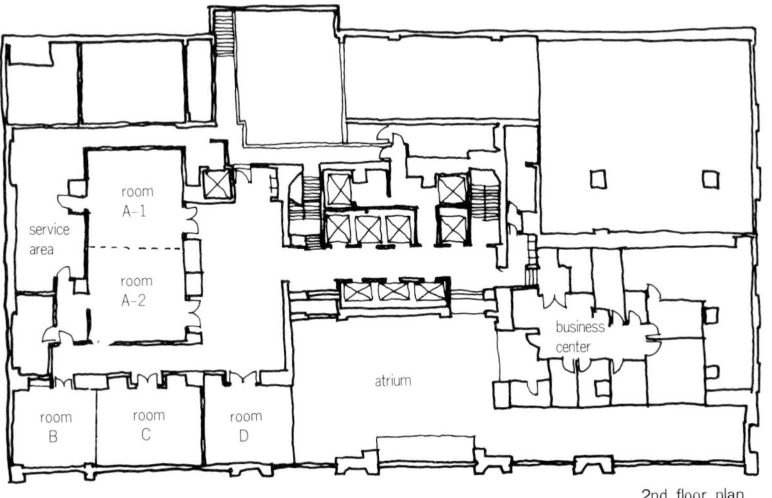

2nd floor plan

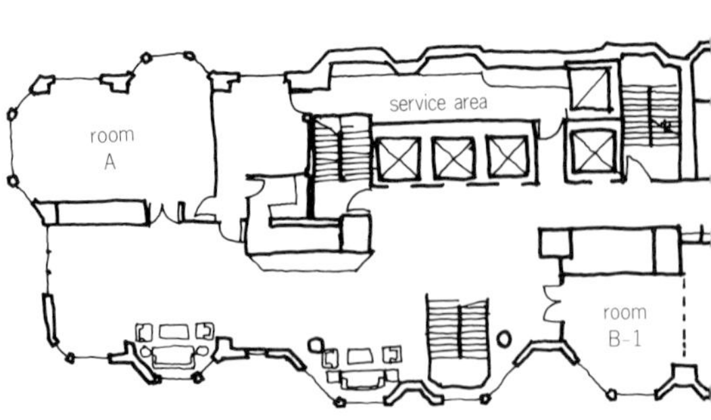

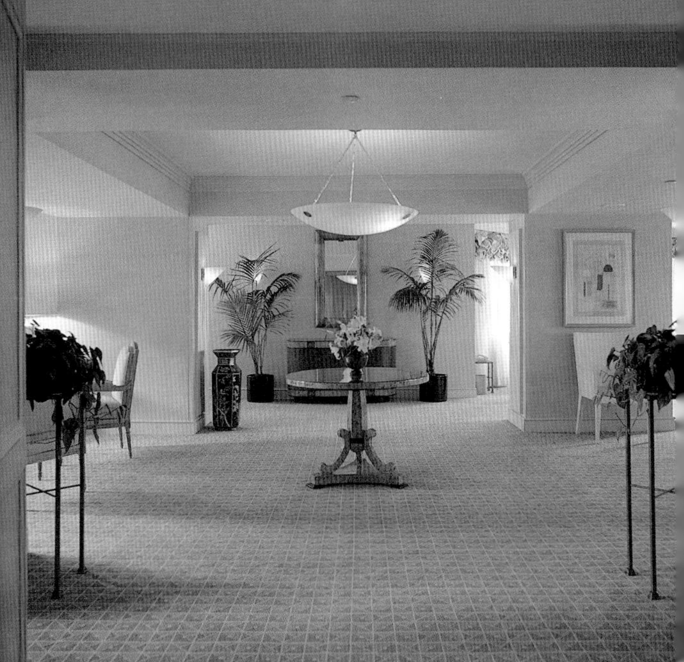

上/100人収容のバンケットルーム　最上階にあり見晴しの良さをセールスポイントにしている
下/エレベーターホール近くの通路を利用したレセプション

Top / The banquet room accommodating 100 persons; occupying the highest floor, it features a beautiful view.
Bottom / The reception utilizing the aisle near the elevator hall.

上/53階のボードルーム　ハドソン川やセントラルパークを見下せるコーナー
下/ホスピタリティ スイートのエントランスからみる中央部　両サイドには4つのオープンな多目的の会議 宴会場がある

Top / The boardroom on the 53rd floor; from this corner one can overlook the Hudson, Central Park, etc.
Bottom / Hospitality; the central part viewed from the entrance of the suite room. On both sides there are 4 open-type multi-purpose conference and banquet halls.

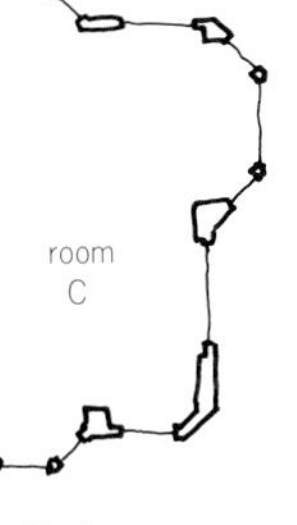

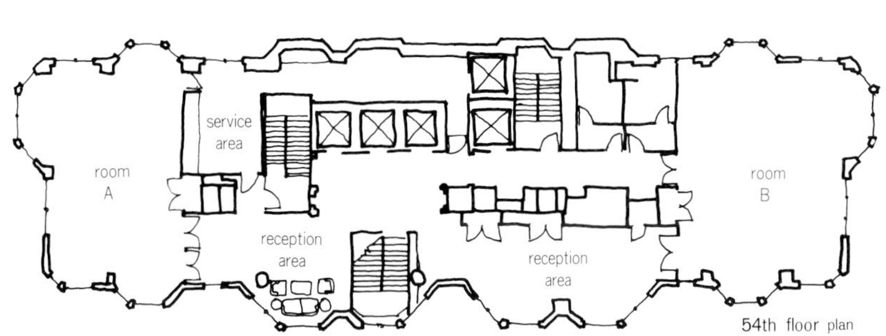

ミラーのあるフレンチドアで仕切る　スイート ルームのリビング ルームとベッド ルーム

The living room and bedroom of the suite room.

八角形の細長いリビング ルームは8人までの会合ができる

The slender octagonal living room can be used for a meeting of up to 8 persons.

シャワー ルーム付のバスルーム

The bathroom with a shower room.

グランド ロイヤル スイートのエメラルドグリーンを強調したマスター ベッドルーム
The master's bedroom of the grand royal suite room; stressing emerald green.

上/広いスペースのリビングとダイニング ルームを備えたスイート ルーム
下/キッチンも備えたダイニング ルーム
Top / The suite room equipped with spacious living and dining rooms.
Bottom / The dining room is also equipped with a kitchen.

見晴しの良い　豪華な雰囲気のグランド ロイヤル スイートのバスルーム
The gorgeous bathroom of the grand royal suite room from which one can command a fine view.

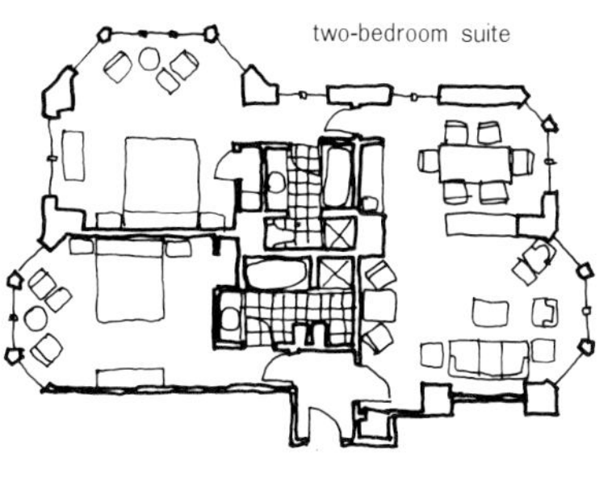

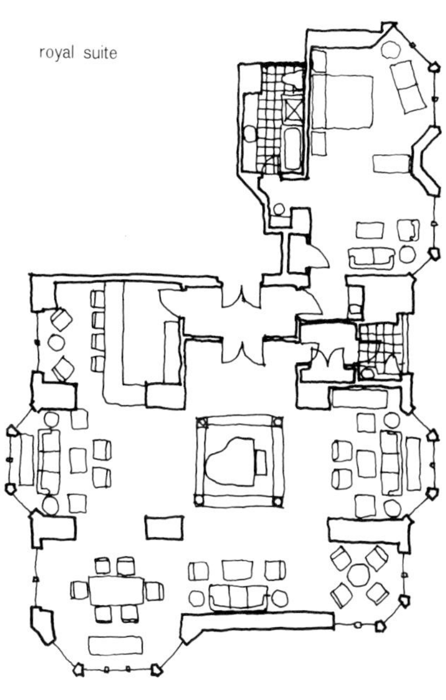

2階会議室のエレベーター ホール

The elevator hall of the 2nd floor conference room.

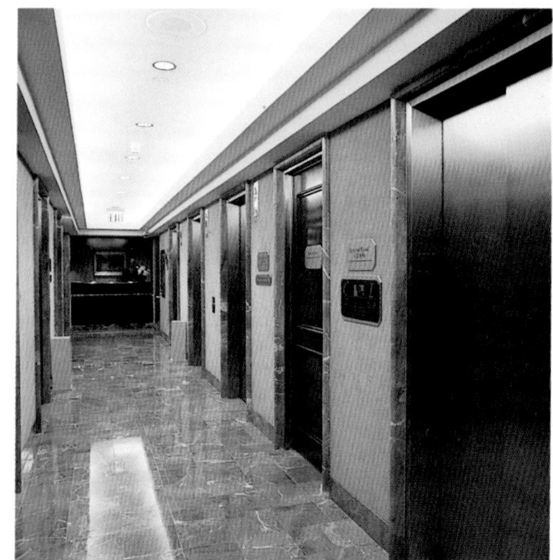

1階エレベーター ホール

The 1st floor elevator hall.

フィットネス センター

The fitness center.

上/スタジオを思わせるエレベーター ホール前のロビー
左下/ホテルには有名な「PALACE」シアターとホテル専用の入口がある
右下/タイムズ スクエアに面して建つ43階　460室の外観

Top / The lobby in front of the elevator hall looks like a studio.
Left, bottom / Apart from its own entrance, the hotel has also an entrance to the famous "PALACE" theater.
Right, bottom / The appearance of the 43-storied hotel with 460 rooms facing the Times Square.

EMBASSY SUITES HOTEL

1568 Broadway New York, N.Y. 10036
Phone/212-719-1600

広いエレベーター ホール前の白と黒の幾何学模様フロア
The black & white geometrically patterned floor in front of the spacious elevator hall.

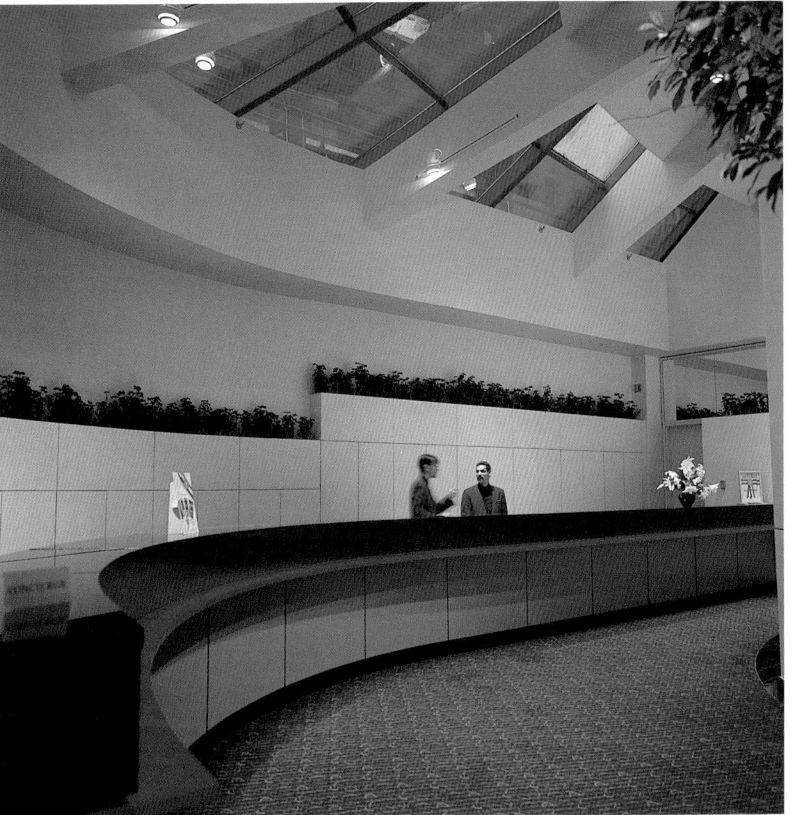

上/スカイライトのあるロビーとコンシアージ デスク
下/円形のレセプション

Top / The skylighted lobby and concierge desk.
Bottom / The round reception.

ロビーの吹抜け部のアートワーク

The artwork in the stairwell area of the lobby.

EMBASSY SUITES HOTEL

Just as the name suggests, all of guest rooms are suites composed of a bedroom and living room, but can be used at economy rates, so that the hotel is very popular. At present, the "Embassy Suites Hotel" chain is operating chain hotels at about 120 locations across America, but has advanced into New York City for the first time. Although New York is yearly visited by about 20 million tourists, the hotel has improved its equipment mainly intended for businessmen. The hotel prepares its guide, menu, etc. not merely in English, but also in German, French, Japanese, Italian and Spanish, and it also has a week-end package plan for family guests. Featuring an art deco design, each room has as standard equipment one TV set and a two-circuit multifunction telephone (with an auto message hold button; connectable with a computer and fax set) in both the living room and bedroom, it also has a wet bar, refrigerator, microwave oven, coffee maker, etc. Breakfast is served in a buffet style, and guests can request eggs, etc. to be cooked as they desire. The cocktail reception held by the manager everyday for 2 hours from 5:30 p.m. is very popular, since guests can enjoy the free drinks they prefer. The time-honored "Palace Theater" preserved on the 1st floor of the hotel has been repaired and reopened.

Opened : September 1990

Scale · number of rooms: 43 stories above the ground; 460 rooms

Eating & drinking facilities: Fosses (piano bar occupying 2 floors)/ Deco 30 (Continental Restaurant & Lounge)

Banquet & conference facilities: 2,050 sq. feet (accommodates 350 persons)/conference suite rooms 12 (each with a board-room and bedroom)/conference rooms 6/boardrooms (360 sq. feet each) 2

Other facilities: Training room (850 sq. feet)

Standard guest room equipment: Composition/bedroom × 1 and living room × 1 (with breakfast and also cocktail reception invited by manager); TV set × 2, multifunction telephone × 3 (with auto message hold button; connectable with computer and fax set); others/dining table, wet bar, microwave oven, refrigerator and coffee maker.

エンバシー スイート ホテル

名前のとおり全客室がベッドルームとリビングルームで構成されたスイートルームでありながら エコノミー料金で宿泊できるこのホテルは大変な人気である。現在アメリカ中の約120カ所にチェーン展開しているが ニューヨーク シティへは初めての進出である。1年間に約2,000万人の旅行者が訪れるニューヨークであるが このホテルでは特にビジネスマンたちを対象にし 設備を充実させている。英語の他に独 仏 日 伊 スペイン語のホテル案内やメニューが用意され ウイークエンドには家族向けのパッケージプランもある。アートデコのデザインが取り入れられ 客室には2台のTVセット 2回線多機能電話(オートメッセージ ホールドボタン付き コンピューター及びファックス接続可能)がリビングとベッドルーム バスルームに各1台ずつ置かれている。更に ウエットバーと冷蔵庫 マイクロウエーブ オーブン。コーヒーメーカーなども標準装備されている。朝食はビュッフェ形式で 卵など希望に応じて料理してくれる。毎日午後の5時30分から2時間 マネージャーが招待するカクテル レセプションが行われ 無料で好みのドリンクスを楽しめるのも大変な人気である。ホテルの1階には由緒のある「パレス シアター」が保存改修されオープンしている。

開　　　業：1990年9月
規模・客室数：地上43階 460室
料 飲 施 設：Fosses(2フロアのピアノバー)/Deco 30(コンチネンタル レストラン&ラウンジ)
宴会・会議室：2,050sq, feet(350名収容)/コンファレンス スイート 12室(ボードルーム及び ベッドルーム付き)/会議室 6室/ボードルーム(360sq, feet) 2室
その他施設：トレーニングルーム(850sq, feet)
客室の標準設備：構成/1ベッドルーム 1リビングルーム(朝食付き マネージャー招待によるカクテル レセプションあり) TVセット/2台 多機能電話/3台(オートメッセージ ホールドボタン付き コンピューター&ファックス接続可能) その他/ダイニングテーブル ウエットバー マイクロウエーブオーブン 冷蔵庫及びコーヒーメーカー

上/44フィートのスカイロビーとエレベーター ホール
下/パイプをあしらったエレベーター ホール

Top/The sky lobby (44 feet long) and elevator hall.
Bottom/The elevator hall accented with pipes.

ジャズ ピアノ バー「Fosse's」(5階)

The jazz piano bar "FOSSE'S" (5th floor).

「Fosse's」のエントランス

The entrance to "FOSSE'S."

2つのフロアで構成するクラブ風のピアノ バー

The piano bar composed of 2 floors; looking like a club.

マネジャーが宿泊客を招待し毎夕開くレセプションは　このホテルチェーンの特色

The reception held every evening by the manager inviting guests is another feature of the hotel chain.

レセプションの催されるスペース

The space where the reception is held.

レセプションの催される上階のラウンジ

The upper floor lounge used for the reception.

5階にある レストランとバー「Deco 30」

The restaurant and bar "DECO 30" on the 5th floor.

「Deco 30」のエントランス ホール

The entrance hall of "DECO 30."

朝食時は このカウンターをビュッフェ テーブルとして利用する

During breakfast time this counter is used as a buffet table.

350人収容できる宴会場は3つに仕切れる

The banquet hall capable of accommodating 350 persons can be partitioned into three parts.

重装備のフィットネス センター

The heavily equipped fitness center.

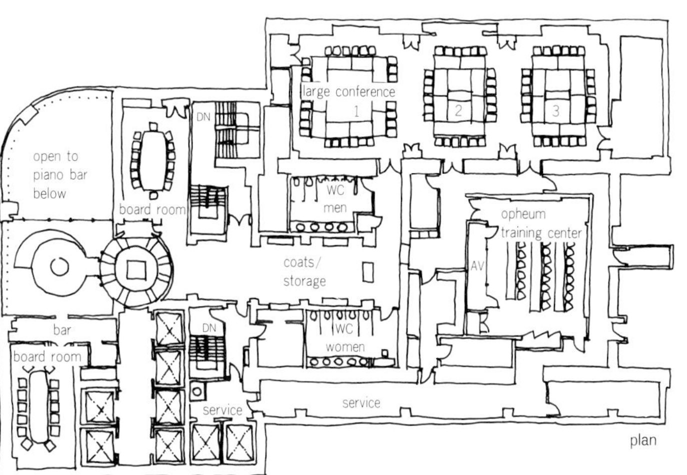

客室はリビングやベッドルームの他にミニバー　コーヒーメーカー　マイクロウェーブ オーブンなども完備している
Each guest room is equipped not merely with a living room and bedroom, but also a mini bar, coffee maker, microwave oven, etc.

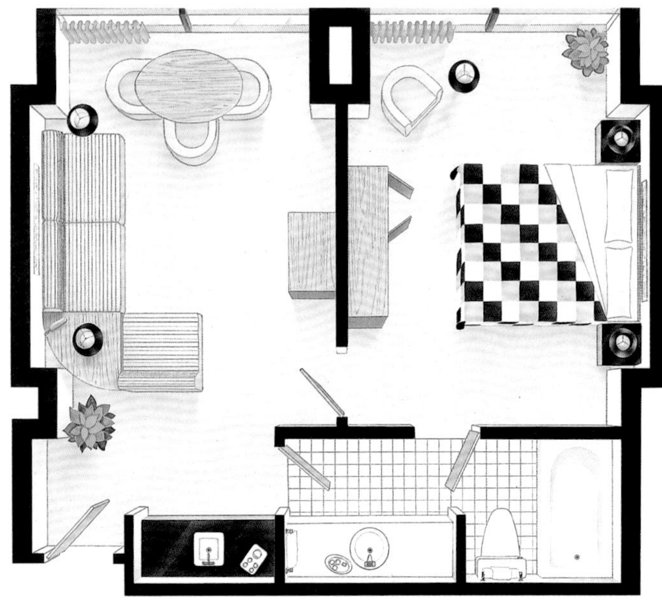

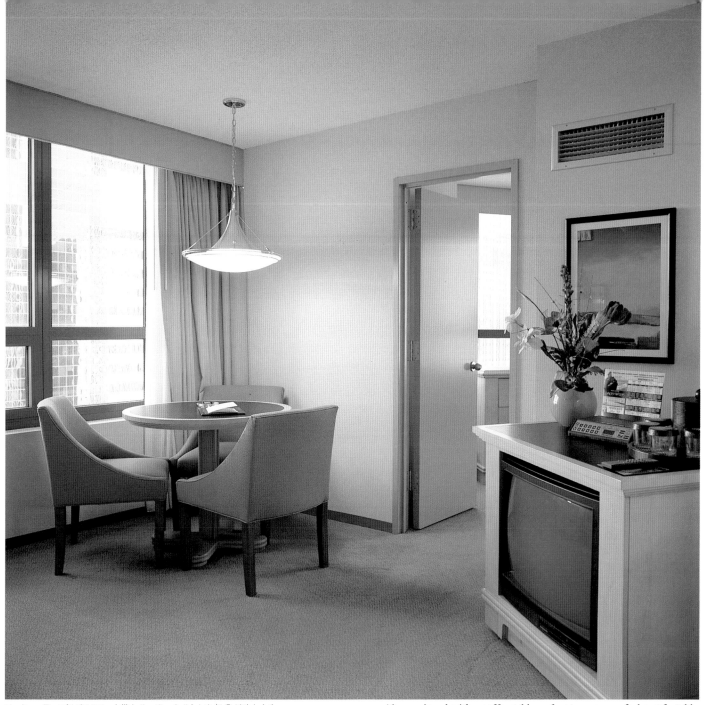

コーヒー テーブルやソファも備わり ゆったりとした気分が味わえる

Also equipped with a coffee table, sofa, etc., one can feel comfortable.

左/キング サイズのベッド ルーム

Left / The king-size bedroom.

プレジデンシャル スイートのリビングルーム

The living room of the presidential suite room.

スイート ルームの入口より客室をみる

A guest room viewed from the entrance of the suite room.

各ルームには3台の多機能電話があり　ビジネスマンたちに重宝がられているれている

Each room is equipped with 3 multifunction telephones which are conveniently used by businessmen.